D1553746

While reading Sharon Betters's p
privilege of God-glorifying, Spir
agement, my heart was arrested. I closed the book to contact a hurting friend. *Treasures of Encouragement* has the potential to transform churches into powerhouses of Christ's compassion and love. May it be so!

—**Leslie Bennett**, Speaker, Author, *Leader Connection* (Blog) Content Manager, *Revive Our Hearts*; Editor, *Women's Ministry Leader Survival Guide* and *10 Truths to Set Leaders Free*

Treasures of Encouragement is a timely reminder of the power of God's Word to change a life and to make the impossible doable. I appreciated the encouragement to look around and see that I have a part in helping the Lord to comfort the wounded and restore the hurting. I heartily recommend this book to anyone who wants to experience more of the grace of God.

—**Annie Chapman**, Singer; Speaker; Author, *Letting Go of Anger* and *The Mother-in-Law Dance*

Out of personal and profound grief, Sharon Betters has written a classic that is a must-have for every Christian's library. In it, she lays out the essential aspects of a church whose culture is fueled by biblical encouragement and shows what it means to be part of a congregation that is a safe place of grace—that allows Christians to make mistakes, fall down, get up, and continue to grow together in Christ.

—**Melanie Cogdill**, General Editor, *Beyond the Roles*; Member, The Pelican Project

Biblical encouragers helped me to climb out of a dark depression, so I love how this book reminds readers that all God's children are called to be encouragers. In a self-centered and broken world, the combination of real-life personal stories and biblical focus reminds us that coming alongside one another is a privilege. I am grateful for the emphasis Sharon places on the power of Scripture to comfort others when we don't know what to say. I hope that many read this book and know that they too are equipped and called to be God's promise keepers through the practice of biblical encouragement.

—**Jan Dravecky**, Cofounder, Endurance with Jan and Dave Dravecky; Author; Speaker

Encouragement is a gift, a treasure both to give and to receive from the body of Christ. Sharon Betters unpacks what this biblical encouragement looks like in the life of a believer. Using personal stories of those who entered into her own sorrow or who received this treasure from the godly, as well as Christ-centered teaching from Scripture, Betters equips readers to walk beside the hurting. May we show the world who Christ is as we encourage one another with the mutual hope we have in Christ.

—**Christina Fox**, Counselor; Speaker; Author, *Closer Than a Sister*

With practical wisdom that nourishes the parched and brittle soul, Sharon introduces us to real women with real struggles. Through their stories she challenges us to think biblically about our own struggles while infusing the hope needed to navigate them.

—**Vanessa K. Hawkins**, Director of Women's Ministry, First Presbyterian Church, Augusta, Georgia; Speaker; Cohost, *Something to Talk About* podcast

To encourage is to inspire courage, hope, or confidence. Twenty-five years ago, I picked up *Treasures of Encouragement* as a young pastor's wife who was desperately looking for these comforts. The truths contained within these covers have stood the test of time and personally sustained me. I am delighted to endorse this new edition of *Treasures of Encouragement.*

—**Karen Hodge**, Coordinator of Women's Ministries, Presbyterian Church in America; Author, *Transformed* and *Life-giving Leadership*

Sharon's theological integrity and her personal pilgrimage through pain harmonize into a glorious doxology.
—**Susan Hunt**, Author, *Spiritual Mothering* and *Aging with Grace*

People often ask me how to walk alongside friends who are hurting. Practical, honest, and steeped in Scripture, this book provides better answers than anything else I have read. I have turned to it again and again, both for comfort in my own suffering as well as for ideas for ministering to others. I read the original twenty-three years ago, shortly after my son died, and it was truly a treasure of encouragement to me. Sharon's words shaped my thinking and helped me to press into the Lord as I wrestled with questions, doubts, and fear. I am indebted to her for this work, and after you read *Treasures of Encouragement*, you will be too. I highly recommend it!
—**Vaneetha Rendall Risner**, Author, *Walking through Fire* and *The Scars That Have Shaped Me*

Deeply moving, compelling, and extremely practical.
—**Stephen Smallman**, Author, *Beginnings* and *The Walk*

Sharon Betters taught me about lament. This book is a discipleship treasure for practical encouragement in hard seasons. It equipped junior-high girls to boldly serve one another and me when my sister passed away. *Treasures of Encouragement* still gives me courage. I am a debtor to the way God faithfully uses Sharon's suffering by His mercy for the ministry of encouragement in my life.
—**Barbara Thompson**, Author, *Equipping the Church for Kingdom Prayer*; Coauthor, *The Legacy of Biblical Womanhood*

TREASURES OF *Encouragement*

WOMEN HELPING WOMEN

SHARON W. BETTERS

P&R
PUBLISHING
P.O. BOX 817 • PHILLIPSBURG • NEW JERSEY 08865-0817

A leader's guide for this book is available at the PCA Bookstore (www.pcabookstore.com).

© 1996, 2021 by Sharon W. Betters

First edition 1996
Second edition 2021

All rights reserved. No part of this book may be reproduced, stored in a retrieval system, or transmitted in any form or by any means—electronic, mechanical, photocopy, recording, or otherwise—except for brief quotations for the purpose of review or comment, without the prior permission of the publisher, P&R Publishing Company, P.O. Box 817, Phillipsburg, New Jersey 08865-0817.

Unless otherwise indicated, all Scripture quotations are from the HOLY BIBLE, NEW INTERNATIONAL VERSION. Copyright © 1973, 1978, 1984 International Bible Society. Used by permission of Zondervan Bible Publishers.

Unless the text indicates that they are the author's own, Scripture quotations marked "Amplified" are taken from the Amplified® Bible (AMPC), Copyright © 1954, 1958, 1962, 1964, 1965, 1987 by The Lockman Foundation. Used by permission. www.lockman.org

Scripture quotations marked (NKJV) are taken from the New King James Version®. Copyright © 1982 by Thomas Nelson. Used by permission. All rights reserved.

Italics within Scripture quotations indicate emphasis added.

Cover design by Rebecca Mercer

ISBN: 978-1-62995-881-1 (pbk)

Printed in the United States of America

Library of Congress Control Number: 2021935788

This book is written with thanksgiving to God for my greatest earthly encourager, Chuck, whose lifetime hunger and thirst for God's righteousness encouraged our son Mark to prepare for the greatest experience of his life— to be with Jesus and to be like Jesus.

And for my friend, Diane Walker

From the first day we met to the day she stepped into heaven thirty-one years later, Diane taught me the meaning of biblical encouragement. She loved me unconditionally and refused to leave my side in the darkest days. I know she is in that great cloud of witnesses, continuing to cheer on her loved ones and me.

"I will go before you and will level the mountains; I will break down gates of bronze and cut through bars of iron. I will give you the treasures of darkness, riches stored in secret places, so that you may know that I am the Lord, the God of Israel, who summons you by name."
(Isaiah 45:2–3)

CONTENTS

FOREWORD

It's one thing to write a book. It's another thing to live the principles in the book for twenty-five years after it is published. The ministry of encouragement is still the passion of Sharon's life.

This book was written in the crucible of suffering after the death of Sharon's sixteen-year-old son Mark and his friend Kelly in an automobile accident. At the time of the accident, Sharon was on our women's ministry leadership committee for the Presbyterian Church in America. The women on this committee lived in different parts of the country but our hearts were connected by our love for the Lord, His Word, and His church and by our desire to equip women to live for God's glory. We were gospel friends. It was agonizing to watch our friend grieve. Her grief was deep. It was raw. Sometimes it was scary. But deep in my soul I believed God would bring light from the darkness to guide others. The first time I said this out loud to Sharon, she responded, "I don't want to help others; I want Mark back." I had spoken too quickly. I needed someone to teach me to be an encourager.

In time, our conversations were sprinkled with ways she was experiencing encouragement from others and how sometimes the silence of others discouraged her deeply. We concluded that silence is usually the result of not knowing what to do or say. Through it all, the dominant theme I heard from Sharon was how the Lord was encouraging her through His Word. My heart longed for her to help me to understand the treasures in the darkness (Isaiah 45:2–3) she was discovering. I began to see a glimmer of desire in her to help women in the church to know how to encourage others. Our committee trembled when we asked her to write a book on encouragement because we knew we were asking for a costly gift.

Sharon gave us practical ways to be encouragers, and she gave us a biblical reason to be encouragers. She taught us to think biblically about the ministry of encouragement. The result was transformative, for me and countless other women. I am a witness to the beauty of women applying the encouragement of the gospel to the wounds of hurting women and to the covenant community becoming stronger, safer, and sweeter. This book is Sharon's sacrifice of praise. Her theological integrity and her personal pilgrimage through pain harmonize into a glorious doxology.

I'm grateful for this new edition of *Treasures of Encouragement*. I pray the legacy of encouragement will now be given to the next generation of women.

Susan Hunt

INTRODUCTION

On July 6, 1993, our family enjoyed a quiet evening at home—an evening we soon would have forgotten were it not for the events that followed. Ten minutes after our sixteen-year-old son, Mark, and his friend, Kelly, left our home, they died in a car accident.

Shattered by the intrusion of death, I soon learned why Scripture calls it our enemy (1 Corinthians 15:26). Every day brought reminders of Mark's physical absence—an empty bedroom, an untouched jacket, his dog patiently waiting on the bed, his brothers and sister wailing loudly or quietly weeping.

When God's promises of sufficiency, joy, and peace seemed far away and impossible for Him to keep in the aftermath of death's defilement, I found hope in Isaiah 45:2-3:

> I will go before you and will level the mountains; I will break down gates of bronze and cut through bars of iron. I will give you the treasures of darkness, riches stored in secret places, so that you may know that I am the Lord, the God of Israel, who summons you by name.

And I found comfort in Lamentations 3:22-23:

> His compassions never fail. They are new every morning; great is your faithfulness.

The healing balm of encouragement eventually stopped the spread of despair's infection and began replacing it with hope's healthy glow. God's Word was the healing balm, and God's people applied it lavishly to soothe the searing pain in my soul.

Biblical encouragement is soul work. God unleashes its mysterious power every time a child of God follows the Holy Spirit's direction and steps into the suffering of another person. Individuals, families, and churches need it regularly to maintain spiritual health. And both the encouraged and the encourager are changed through its application. Scriptural encouragers invest in their own spiritual welfare every time they give of themselves to another.

Encouragement can be as simple as smiling warmly at an awkward adolescent or as complex as walking through the shadow of death with a disease-ravaged friend. Its power is limitless and its practice is a privilege.

Believers often feel guilty when the need for encouragement is raised. How many times have you lamented, "I know I should be more of an encourager, but . . ." or "I wish someone would encourage me." Rather than reach confidently into our treasure chest of salvation to find just the right encouragement jewel for our child or friend, we selfishly close the lid, hoarding the treasures for ourselves. And we miss the opportunity to make a difference.

The premise of this book is that when Christ is in us, we have the treasures of His encouragement at our fingertips. And when we obey the encouragement mandate, the treasures we give are multiplied in our own lives. It's a win-win situation.

This is not a textbook on encouragement. It is a passionate plea for the lavish use of encouragement. Its application continually restores my soul, and I want others to experience that restoration.

As children of God, we have every tool we need to mend broken hearts and lives. So instead of isolating ourselves in a self-made cocoon of protection, we need to find out what those tools are, learn how to use them, and get to work reviving hope in hurting hearts.

Women who know Christ and the power of His resurrection realize that God does not leave us helpless in the face of difficulty. He miraculously transforms our meager offerings and uses even the simplest acts to bring about dramatic change.

Although this book was written from the crucible of suffering, it is not about grief. It is about how God uses us—His children—to do soul work as we become His promise keepers. It is about the privilege of giving to others from the treasure chest of our salvation. And its purpose is to help women to

- think biblically about their position in Christ
- live biblically as the treasures of encouragement emerge from this new way of thinking

Part 1, "Thinking Biblically," lays the Scriptural foundation for such actions.

Part 2, "Living Biblically," looks at specific ways to encourage. Many women want to encourage but need help in figuring out creative ways to do it.[1] Following part 2 is an addendum of fifty practical encouragement ideas.

Each chapter opens with one or more true encouragement stories. Many women submitted to me their real-life stories, some of which have been edited to protect the privacy of the storyteller. Numerous personal accounts are also scattered throughout the text. Each chapter includes an Encouragement Principle, six days of daily devotions, and a specific way to practice encouragement or cultivate intimacy with Christ. Before reading each chapter, ask God to open your heart to His message for you. Underline, or copy on note cards, the statements that God impresses on your heart as you read and complete the study questions. Journaling your way through the text and Scripture will clarify the encouragement principles and applications to your life. Of course, the more time you take to think through the probing questions, the more impact the study will have on you.

My prayer is for renewed strength in the body of Christ as we begin giving to others the treasures of His encouragement, thus becoming God's promise keepers.

---

1 This book was written for individual readers as well as for small group study. A separate leader's guide expands the material and explains how to lead a small group. It is available through the PCA Bookstore (www.pcabookstore.com).

Part 1

Thinking Biblically

Chapter One

PRICELESS TREASURES OF ENCOURAGEMENT

Aleta's Story

From the time my husband decided to leave me until it actually happened, many close friends tried to encourage me with well-meaning words. "He won't leave," they assured me. "He knows he has a good thing with you. It's a phase!"

Although I appreciated their good intentions, the words rang hollow. I knew that God doesn't always grant happy endings—not even to Christians. My well-intentioned friends had no biblical basis for their reassuring statements.

Then God gave me a friend whose faith of steel had been forged in the heat of tough times. She had an unorthodox response to my story of broken dreams. "Your husband may very well leave you and your children," she said. "So you need to ask yourself, 'Will I trust God to care for us, husband or no husband?'"

The turning point in my fearful journey came when she directed me to submit my raging emotions to the truths and promises of God. Her words set me free because they helped me face reality. She had the courage to step into my pain and to encourage me with the only thing that could help—the truth.

Jane's Story

Chronic pain was affecting me emotionally and spiritually as well as physically. As my body grew tolerant to the medication, doctors increased the dosage from one or two pills a day to eight or ten. But the pain remained the same. The only things that changed were my feelings of loneliness and helplessness; they continued to increase.

Then a special Christian sister stepped into my life. She always seemed to know when to call or send a card. She took me out on Friday nights "just to talk," and she gave me a "joy box" in which I kept many of the treasures of encouragement she sent to me.

My pain finally drove me to search for treatment in a psychiatric hospital. A Christian roommate assured me that God had not abandoned me. I asked God to teach me how to love and serve Him on His terms. I asked Him to take my eyes off of myself and my pain and to help me focus on others. As I diligently prayed for God to teach me how to die to self, I received another special treasure. He eventually removed my physical pain!

The time has come for me to give a "joy box" to someone else and to fill it with treasures of encouragement—the way God, through my friend, encouraged me.

Encouragement Principle 1

God keeps His promises through other believers.

The news was like an explosion in the heart of our home. Our sixteen-year-old son, Mark, and his girlfriend, Kelly, had been killed. The darkest night of my soul had begun. God's promises mocked my sorrow. How could I ever trust Him again?

The answer came through a body of believers who functioned as God's promise keepers. Feeling betrayed by God, I refused to acknowledge His love for me, but God demonstrated that love through His physical representation on earth—the church.

From the moment people learned of Mark's death, they began sending cards and personal notes of encouragement. These along with their gifts of practical service were our lifeline to the reality of God's character.

Before Mark's death I had taught for many years on the subject of encouragement, but my beliefs had never been tested in the laboratory of grief. My own experience caused me to wonder how many people in the body of Christ have not healed from life's devastating blows simply because the other members of the body are not fulfilling their duty to encourage.

Because my husband was the pastor of our church, we received much support. Many people stretched themselves to find ways to minister to us. Others, however, treated us as if we were lepers. And some of those who avoided us were people I thought would never let us down. Why? There had to be a good reason.

I had to look only as far as my own life to find clues, for I am not innocent in the disregard of encouragement. Sometimes I am caring and sensitive. I send cards with special notes, make phone calls, take a meal to a housebound mom, greet the newly widowed with a hug, and speak encouragingly to my husband and children.

At other times, however, I am not such a good friend. I neglect to send a card, acknowledge the death of a loved one, or hug the parent of a rebellious child. I guide conversations away from deep needs toward trivial matters, and I even forget my promises to pray. The longer I neglect the need, the more embarrassed I am to see the friend I disappointed.

Why do I disregard such simple means of encouragement? Why do so many others refuse to get involved beyond a superficial level in the lives of struggling believers? Why do we often view these commands as drudgery and resent obeying them? Why do we neglect such a great opportunity? Five reasons come to mind:

1. *Our own lives are full of urgent demands.*

2. *We don't know what to say or do, so we decide it is better to say or do nothing than to say or do the wrong thing.*

3. *We give up when our initial efforts show no results.*

4. *We are insensitive.*

These explanations are all variations of the one real reason we fail to encourage one another:

5. *We do not understand our identity in Christ.*

As our understanding of our stature as God's children increases, our reasons for failing to encourage others fall away. When the Word of God defines our identity and when our intimacy with Christ determines our character, not only will we know how to display God's love to others, we will desire to do so as well.

Rather than risk intimacy with Christ, however, we try to pass the buck. To ease the guilt of noninvolvement, we charge the church with the job of meeting needs. We forget that we are the church!

In congregations where believers think of their church as a living organism—a body—rather than as just an institution, the church pulsates with hope and healing. When church members practice the ministry of encouragement that flows from intimacy with Christ, the church becomes a healing place for wounded believers and a magnet to seekers.

The Meaning of Encouragement

One dictionary[1] defines *encourage* this way: "To give courage, spirit, or hope; to stimulate."

Courage: "Mental or moral strength to venture, persevere, and withstand danger, fear, or difficulty."

Spirit: "The activating or essential principle influencing a person."

Hope: "A desire accompanied by expectation of or belief in fulfillment."

Stimulate: "To excite to activity or growth."

Imagine being able to affect another person in such a powerful way. Many people today would have us believe that we can accom-

1 *Merriam Webster's Collegiate Dictionary*, 10th ed. (Springfield, Mass.: Merriam-Webster, Inc., 1994).

plish this with warm words and fuzzy feelings, but the scriptural practice of encouragement demands much more. Scriptural encouragement is ongoing, daily, and consistent. It requires perseverance, and it includes the following practices:

Strengthening: "And we urge you, brothers, warn those who are idle, encourage the timid, help the weak, be patient with everyone" (1 Thessalonians 5:14)

Motivating: "Now go out and encourage your men. I swear by the Lord that if you don't go out, not a man will be left with you by nightfall. This will be worse for you than all the calamities that have come upon you from your youth till now" (2 Samuel 19:7).

Assuring: "But your assistant, Joshua son of Nun, will enter it. Encourage him, because he will lead Israel to inherit it" (Deuteronomy 1:38).

Exhorting: "When he arrived and saw the evidence of the grace of God, he was glad and encouraged them all to remain true to the Lord with all their hearts" (Acts 11:23).

Supporting: ". . . learn to do right! Seek justice, encourage the oppressed. Defend the cause of the fatherless, plead the case of the widow" (Isaiah 1:17).

Disciplining: "See to it, brothers, that none of you has a sinful, unbelieving heart that turns away from the living God. But encourage one another daily, as long as it is called Today, so that none of you may be hardened by sin's deceitfulness. We have come to share in Christ if we hold firmly till the end the confidence we had at first. As has just been said: 'Today, if you hear his voice, do not harden your hearts as you did in the rebellion'" (Hebrews 3:12–15).

True encouragement pumps hope into the receiver and also into the giver.

God's Promise Keepers

When I was reeling from those haunting words, "Your son is dead," how could I believe promises like this one in Hebrews: "God has said, 'Never will I leave you; never will I forsake you'" (13:5)? In fact, how could I believe any of God's other promises of security?

In the dark periods of life it is difficult to believe that God will keep His many promises. But He does, and He often does it through other believers whom He enables and charges with the responsibility of encouraging one another.

Long before the now-popular Promise Keepers' men's movement entered the scene, God established that *all* His children would be promise keepers—*His* promise keepers.

Consider 2 Corinthians 1:3–5:

> Praise be to the God and Father of our Lord Jesus Christ, the Father of compassion and the God of all comfort, who comforts us in all our troubles, so that we can comfort those in any trouble with the comfort we ourselves have received from God. For just as the sufferings of Christ flow over into our lives, so also through Christ our comfort overflows.

God's compassion streaming through us and into others is His "divine solution" to the problems of discouragement, grief, and sorrow. God holds the members of His body responsible for making sure that other members experience His love:

> A new command I give you: Love one another. As I have loved you, so you must love one another. By this all men will know that you are my disciples, if you love one another. (John 13:34–35)

When I was grieving the death of my son, the faithfulness of other believers soothed my hurting heart. When members of His body were faithful and entered my pain, God used their sensitive words, hugs, tears, and practical acts of service to demonstrate His presence. Without it, healing would have taken much longer. I imagined God saying to members of the body, *Sharon is missing Mark and feeling abandoned by Me. I promised her I would never forsake her, but grief blinds her to My presence. Be My ambassador and let Me love her through you. Write her a note, share your memories of Mark, pray for her right now. Be My promise keeper for this moment.*

God calls us to encourage those caught in the daily grind of life as well as those in crisis.

Consider the single mother overwhelmed by all the responsibilities resting on her. What is she thinking as she reads, "For this God is our God for ever and ever; he will be our guide even to the end" (Psalm 48:14) and "I am the Lord, your God, who takes hold of your right hand and says to you, Do not fear; I will help you" (Isaiah 41:13).

God can keep His promise to guide her; the wisdom she finds in His Word can keep her headed in the right direction. But how does He take hold of her right hand and tell her not to be afraid? He does it through other believers. He wants and expects our cooperation.

God commands older women to teach younger women how to live (Titus 2:3–5), and an important aspect of teaching is encouragement. Young women need the assurance that they are not alone and that they are doing many things right. I can imagine God prompting a mature believer with thoughts like this one: *That young mom is overwhelmed. Her fear of the unknown is all she can see. The sound of shattering dreams has made her deaf to My Word. Let her know she is not alone. Let My wisdom and love flow through you to her. Represent Me by helping her with the children or inviting her to dinner. Be My promise keeper for this hour in her life.*

My son's kindergarten teacher encouraged me with this kind of hope during a particularly difficult stage in my son's life. "Sharon," she said, "my son is older now, so believe me when I say, 'this too shall pass!'" With those few words, she calmed my fear, not with empty promises, but with knowledge from her own experience. God used her to guide me through the maze of parenting.

The miracle of encouragement is that God can use even simple acts to effect dramatic change. A smile, a kind word, a touch on the shoulder. When those gestures emanate from a heart that truly wants to emulate Christ, the Holy Spirit uses them to instill courage, spirit, and hope—both in the receiver and in the giver.

In my own journey through grief, every act of kindness toward me and my family was a brick on the pathway leading toward God.

No one could take away our pain, but God used each block of encouragement, no matter how small the giver thought it was, to take us one step closer to His healing.

But sometimes encouragement calls for more than a smile, a note, or a kind word. Sometimes it calls for commitment and sacrifice.

Why We Encourage

The ministry of encouragement requires a deep and personal relationship to Jesus Christ, and it demands a lifestyle of servanthood that is rooted in the Incarnation. Authentic scriptural encouragement is a response to God's work in our lives. Because of what Christ has done for us, we are to encourage others (Hebrews 10:24–25). In Philippians 2:1–4 Paul instructs the church to respond to one another with humility and love *because of the comfort of the love of Jesus*. He tells the Thessalonians to "Encourage one another with these words" (1 Thessalonians 4:18). What words? The promise of eternity with the Lord.

Hebrews 10 tells us that the foundation for the ministry of encouragement is our own redemption. Because we have been forgiven, "there is no longer any sacrifice for sin. Therefore, . . . since we have confidence to enter the Most Holy Place by the blood of Jesus, . . . let us consider how we may spur one another toward love and good deeds. Let us not give up meeting together . . . but let us encourage one another" (Hebrews 10:18–25).

The word *consider* (v. 24) means "to observe fully: behold, discover, perceive." This is not a description of a superficial relationship or a quick fix. Biblical encouragement requires time and effort. In response to God's great love for us, we will get to know others so we can discern the best way to stimulate them to reflect the character of Christ. Our motive in encouragement is their good, not ours.

The Greek word translated *spur* (v. 24) in the NIV is *paroxuno*, which means "to sharpen alongside." To help people reach their potential as children of God requires that we come "alongside" of them. This is the same ministry as that of our Comforter, the Holy Spirit, who comes alongside as our encourager. Proverbs speaks of this principle: "As iron sharpens iron, so one man sharpens another" (27:17).

The phrase *give up* (v. 25) means "to leave behind in some place" or "to desert." In other words, we must not desert those who lag behind. We are responsible for one another's well-being.

Gail MacDonald writes about how Jesus encouraged His disciples:

> Jesus prepared the way for these men by going before them at important moments in their lives together. He saw to it that the Upper Room was arranged in order that they might enjoy strength-giving fellowship. After they had failed, he made sure they received the message that he would go ahead of them and meet them in Galilee. This message was especially to be delivered word-of-mouth to Peter because he would need comfort more than anyone. Later, after another night of failure, the Lord was kind enough to prepare a breakfast for a group of tired and chilly fisherman/disciples before they reached the shore. And he has gone before us all to prepare a home in heaven. Could one of the reasons we find being a comforter-friend so difficult today be the time and forethought it requires—time and forethought we are unable or unwilling to give?[2]

The miracle of encouragement takes place as we develop intimacy with Christ. Intimacy with Him teaches us the importance of connecting with one another, which naturally will lead us into deeper and more meaningful relationships. The spiritual needs of people in our circle of influence are made clear as a result of our time spent with Christ.

Imagine the unity and public testimony of churches if obedience to Hebrews 10:24 were the norm: "And let us consider how we may spur one another on toward love and good deeds." Instead of

2 Gail MacDonald, *A Step Farther and Higher* (Portland, Ore.: Multnomah, 1993), 180.

demeaning a volunteer for doing an inadequate job, we will search for a place where she can succeed. Imagine the harmony in our homes if we were to give encouragement a place of prominence. Think of what might happen if smiles and hugs for a moody teenager were a more natural response than critical words.

The possibilities for positive influence are endless.

The Poke Cake

The recipe for the once-popular "poke cake" calls for poking holes in a baked cake and pouring liquid, flavored gelatin over the top. The color and flavor of the gelatin penetrate the cake in a way that is similar to how the life of Jesus permeates our lives. The time we spend with Him in His Word and in His service are the holes into which His Spirit pours His character. When our lives are broken and given in service to others, the vibrant attributes of Christ add beauty and flavor to our own bland nature.

Time spent listening to God, seeking His wisdom, talking to Him, obeying Him, and stepping out by faith to encourage others will cultivate intimacy with Christ and result in His character being revealed in us. When our obedience flows from a deepening awareness of our position in Christ, His presence in us will be evident to those around us.

The finished work of Christ is our motivation. Through the ministry of encouragement, we offer to others what we have found in Him.

If you cooperate in this lifelong process, do not be surprised someday when a friend tells you about words you do not remember speaking that changed her life and set her heart toward God. Do not be surprised when a friend reveals that your quiet presence, at a time when you felt helpless in the face of her great calamity, gave her a sense of peace and the joy of God's nearness.

In the horrendous grief I experienced after the death of my son and his friend, the body of Christ became God's physical arms, holding me tightly in His grip. God gave me the treasure of their scriptural encouragement, forcing me to acknowledge His faithfulness, drawing me from dark anger and sorrow into the glimmering light of His eyes of love.

Throughout this book you will read stories about people whose lives radically changed when someone obeyed the Holy Spirit and encouraged them. Will you listen and offer to another person the treasure of encouragement? Will you be God's promise keeper?

Getting Focused

1. Define encouragement.
2. How do you encourage others?
3. What encourages you?

Staying Focused

Day One

1. Read John 15:1–17. Jesus calls on each of us to bear fruit. What is the prerequisite for bearing fruit? (v. 4)
2. What is the motivation for bearing fruit? (vv. 9–10)
3. What changes in your life will you make to cultivate your relationship to Christ?

Day Two

1. Read Ephesians 3:7–21. What was the driving force in Paul's life? (vv. 7–9)
2. What is God's purpose for the church? (vv. 10–11)
3. Who is the church?
4. In your circle of influence how are you fulfilling God's purpose for the church?
5. Paul says, "For this reason I kneel before the Father" (v. 14). Why did Paul pray?
6. What did Paul pray? (vv. 16–20)
7. Using Paul's prayer as a guide, write out a prayer for yourself. (For example, "Because of the great gift of salvation, I pray that your glorious riches will strengthen me with power through your Spirit in my inner being.")

Day Three

1. Read Philippians 3:7–16. What is the driving force in Paul's life? (vv. 7–11)
2. Did his passion for God make obedience easy or perfect? (vv. 12–14)
3. People often rationalize their refusal to serve God because they feel inadequate. Paul's response to that excuse might be: "Only let us live up to what we have already attained" (v. 16). Are you obeying what you already know?
4. How should what you already know about Christ's accomplishments affect your ministry of encouragement?
5. Who will you encourage today? Write a brief statement about how Christ, through you, can encourage that person. Now do it!

Day Four

1. Read Philippians 2:1–18. Paul calls on the Philippians to put aside their own interests in relationships. Why?
2. Ask God to show you what interests you need to put aside in order to serve Him.

Day Five

1. Read Titus 2. Before Paul outlines the godly behavior Titus is to teach, he exhorts him to teach sound doctrine. Why?
2. After Paul outlines some specific aspects of godly behavior, he states, "For the grace of God that brings salvation has appeared to all men" (v. 11). What impact should this truth have on the way we live?
3. What is your motivation for doing good? (vv. 12–14)

Day Six

1. Read John 13:34–35. How has Jesus loved you? Be specific.
2. How are you loving those in your circle of influence? How will you love them? Be specific!

Living Focused

Reread "Jane's Story—The Gift of the Joy Box." Ask God to bring to mind the name of a person in your circle of influence who needs a "joy box." When you give this gift, commit to filling it with treasures of encouragement—notes, cards, small tokens of love. Allow God to use you to keep His promises to her.

Chapter Two

THE DRIVING FORCE BEHIND ENCOURAGEMENT

Wendy's Story

In my search for contentment, emptiness always followed short-term satisfaction. How was it that I, a Christian, still yearned for something more? To improve my self-image I tried losing weight. But even when I was twenty pounds lighter, my heart was still heavy. When marriage left me discontent, I poured myself into a career, perfecting my work skills to please my bosses. Their pats on the back only made me want more recognition. I searched for meaning and contentment in the ministry of my church. But a full calendar did not fill up the emptiness. My insecurities grew when the praise I received for using my musical talents was never enough. No matter how well I sang, ministered, or worked, I always believed I could have done better.

Thinking self-discipline would make me feel better about myself, I tried exercising. But then doctors diagnosed me with a chronic illness that weakened my body and caused constant muscle pain, making rigorous exercise impossible.

When I decided that having a child surely would bring me fulfillment, a wise counselor realized that I was looking for satisfaction in "doing" rather than in resting in Christ. His counsel saved my future children from the burden of having to fulfill my self-esteem needs.

I began to think about taking my own life, but I was afraid I would botch the attempt and end up with even more problems.

In desperation, I told my husband that I wanted to die. Frightened, he would not let me rest until I agreed to seek counseling.

God used eight weekly sessions to show me the power and reality of Christ in me. Although my circumstances did not change, I began seeking satisfaction in Christ alone. In the months following, I learned to express my feelings to God without fear of judgment. My perfectionism began to melt as I realized that His love for me rested in His character, not in my accomplishment. Seeing Christianity as a relationship rather than a performance enabled me to make decisions that flowed from God's love rather than from my fears of what other Christians would think.

Years later, I am still learning to find fulfillment not in what I do but in the knowledge that I belong to God.

God never restored my physical or emotional strength. Today I live with a chronic illness that has no known cure. My long-term depression sapped the emotional strength that once made me so proud. However, my weaknesses keep my eyes fixed on Jesus, and God uses them to break my bondage to people-pleasing behaviors. Now that I am no longer able to keep up my own daily agenda, I more easily see His.

Instead of measuring my achievement by the numbers of people on my prayer list or the responses I receive to my "good deeds," I let God do the measuring. I have no list now. I simply ask God to let me know who needs encouragement. Then I listen until His Spirit directs me to make a phone call, write a note, or show His love in some creative way. These promptings motivate me to express love, comfort, conviction, and guidance despite how inadequate I feel. The more I respond to His direction, the more direction He gives. God created in me the desire to serve Him and then He gave me the power to do it.

Marybeth's Story

When our choir director asked me to sing a solo in our Christmas cantata, I was both nervous and excited. Uncertainty about my ability kept me in a state of agitation. But God used a compassionate message on my answering machine to encourage me!

Wendy called to tell me that my name had come to mind during her devotion time. Prompted by the Holy Spirit she called to give me encouraging words, share uplifting thoughts, and give my faith a boost. What a great feeling it was to hear my sister in the Lord minister to me. I'm sure her encouragement had much to do with my peacefulness on the night of my solo.

Encouragement Principle 2

We can be God's promise keepers by giving to others from the riches of our inheritance.

The better we understand our position of forgiveness and righteousness in Christ, the more we will want to give to others what we are receiving from Christ. I am passionate about helping women experience the resurrection power that flows from intimacy with Christ regardless of their circumstances. One of the beauties of resurrection power is its unique application to each individual. God does not make cookie-cutter Christians. And when we understand our position in Christ, we are able to express our identity through the unique gifts He gives to each of us. God calls us into a relationship with Him, and it is that relationship which gives us the desire and the ability to obey Him.

The Heart of Obedience

Proverbs repeatedly addresses the issue of how the condition of our hearts (which is the center of our identity) determines our actions:

> Above all else, guard your heart, for it is the wellspring of life. (4:23)

> A heart at peace gives life to the body, but envy rots the bones. (14:30)
>
> A happy heart makes the face cheerful, but heartache crushes the spirit. (15:13)
>
> The heart of the righteous weighs its answers, but the mouth of the wicked gushes evil. (15:28)

According to Psalm 119, the results of obedience are—among other things—delight, freedom, blessing, and rejoicing. Unfortunately, other words sometimes describe my obedience— resentment, anger, and frustration. Many times I have become involved in someone's problems out of guilt or have said "yes" to another job only because pride kept me from saying "no." The result—even though the counseling was given and the job was completed—was a heart filled with resentment. This is not God's plan for His children. Even when obedience is rooted in duty rather than desire, it is still to be considered an "act of worship" (Romans 12:1–2).

When we begin to understand God's love, our passion for Him pushes us beyond our usual limits and causes us to meet people's needs without expecting thanks or credit. Blessings, rejoicing, and delight are eventual side benefits of obedience that flows from a loving heart, rather than from a begrudging spirit.

The familiar New Testament story of Martha and Mary illustrates this important point.

Martha's Story

Tears must have stung Martha's eyes as she helped the servants pick up empty bowls. Her mind raced, searching for the reason her plans for an extraordinary evening with the Master had dissolved into disaster. Jesus and His disciples had needed a place of solitude, and their acceptance of Martha's invitation gave her the opportunity to do what she did best—serve. The aroma of stewed lamb filled the house when they arrived. Bread hot off the coals filled the baskets. Just a few more details and all would be ready. But then everything fell apart. Martha could not be everywhere at once, and Mary, her sister, was not helping! Instead she was sitting at Jesus' feet enjoying His company.

"I'd like to hear His words, too," Martha may have muttered. "But someone has to fix the meal. Jesus doesn't even notice how much I am doing. This is ridiculous." Confident that her indignation was righteous, Martha put her thoughts into words: "Lord, don't you care that my sister has left me to do the work by myself? Tell her to help me!" (Luke 10:40).

Without acknowledging Martha's need for help, Jesus defended Mary's choice, adding confusion and regret to the anger in Martha's soul: "Martha, Martha, you are worried and upset about many things, but only one thing is needed. Mary has chosen what is better, and it will not be taken away from her" (Luke 10:41–42).

What did Jesus mean? Martha was doing what was expected of her and what she believed was right. Why didn't Jesus appreciate it?

Intimacy with Christ

As an orthodox Jewish woman, Martha probably had traditional views of her identity, and she seemed to believe that her sister should hold those views as well. Martha expected Jesus to support her in "reeducating" Mary. Instead Jesus confronted Martha with a fundamental but overlooked truth. Martha wanted Jesus to acknowledge the importance of her service by demanding that Mary behave in the same way, but Jesus defended Mary, saying that she had chosen wisely—that it was important to seize every opportunity to deepen her relationship with Him.

Contemporary thinking and Rabbinic teaching evidently had shaped Martha's view of herself. Josephus, a contemporary of Paul, wrote, "The woman is inferior to the man in every way."[1] Rabbis did not expect women to learn or to understand religious teaching.[2]

1 Contra Apionem, ii 201, quoted in James B. Hurley, *Man and Woman in Biblical Perspective* (Grand Rapids: Zondervan, 1981), 61.

2 For more understanding on this issue, read James B. Hurley, *Man and Woman in Biblical Perspective* (Grand Rapids: Zondervan, 1981) and Susan Hunt, *By Design* (Franklin, Tenn.: Legacy Communications, 1994).

Martha apparently accepted this view, which explains her confusion when Jesus said that her sister had made the better choice. He suggested that Martha's activities, though not inherently bad, nevertheless robbed her of something far more precious.

Martha, by limiting her service to actions that made her comfortable and by demanding that others do likewise, was in danger of making an idol of her traditional role. Jesus, while not discouraging her service, tried to help her focus on something far more important.

A New Way of Seeing

A phenomenon known as Magic Eye has people in malls and bookstores staring at posters, mugs, calendars, and books that claim to have three-dimensional pictures hiding within multi-colored designs. When people see it, they shout, "I see it! I see it!" and everyone else who sees only colored dots feels inferior. I know because I'm one of those who *never* sees it! To see a Magic Eye picture (I am told) you must train yourself to see differently. Children have an easier time than adults because their muscles are more flexible and their way of thinking less rigid. Discovering the hidden object in the Magic Eye picture means learning a new way of seeing. Working at it may make your eyes hurt, but once you see the hidden object, you will have little difficulty seeing it in other designs.

Similarly, Jesus encouraged Martha to see in a new way, to focus on what had previously been hidden to her. To do so, she would have to stop looking at herself and begin exercising weak and seldom used spiritual muscles.

Who Am I?

Jesus uses events in our lives to show us new things about ourselves. Within a year after our son Mark's death, our daughter Heidi married Greg, our son Dan started college, and our oldest son, Chuck, married Melanie. Suddenly I was preparing meals for two instead of six. Every trip to the grocery store reminded me of my changing life. The next two years were to have been Mark's special time as our youngest child; he would have been the center of our attention. My husband and I had planned to use the time to prepare for the imminent empty nest.

Mark's sudden death robbed us of our preparation time and hurled me into an unfamiliar and unwelcome role change. I was forced to reexamine my identity as a woman. Through Mark's death God put me at a frightening crossroad. Would passion for God or the loss of my son become the framework of my identity? Unable to make decisions and impatient with mindless chatter, I retreated from leadership in women's ministry. My inability to function in previous roles raised questions concerning my purpose. Who was I? How should I fill my days? How could I? How would I?

Learning to articulate my ultimate identity as God's disciple rather than as a mother forced me to find new ways of responding to my redemption. Like the excruciating pain of learning to walk again after an injury, every step caused anguish, but my spiritual health demanded that I face the challenge.

What if God's plan for my life includes other losses? What did I have that could not be taken away? Jesus answered this question in His conversation with Martha when He directed her to cultivate her passion for Jehovah. Out of that passion one day would flow service that was more than an obligation; it would be a loving response. Choosing the better part would mean responding out of wholehearted worship, not reluctant duty. Understanding her identity in Christ would change her motivation, though not necessarily her service.

When we meet Martha again, she is face to face with the greatest enemy of man—death. Lazarus, her brother, is dying (John 11:1–44), but this time her message to Jesus reveals increased understanding. In her earlier encounter, she told Jesus how He should handle her sister. But this time she does not demand a specific response. She simply says, "Lord, the one you love is sick" (John 11:3). Certainly Martha expected and hoped that Jesus would hurry to the bedside of her brother and heal him, but her words reveal her belief in His sovereignty.

Jesus, who is bound by no one's desires but God's, took His time traveling to the home of His friends. By the time He arrived, Lazarus had been in the grave for four days.

What were Martha's thoughts as she awaited His arrival? My own struggles to harmonize God's character with the way He sometimes works give me empathy for Martha. She knew Jesus loved Lazarus, but the delay did not fit her definition of love. Concealed in her grief were the pointed words Jesus had spoken to her earlier: "Martha, Martha, you are worried and upset about many things, but only one thing is needed. Mary has chosen what is better, and it will not be taken away from her." Was the key to her relationship with Jesus hidden in those words?

When finally Jesus arrived, Martha's belief in His sovereignty rang out in her exclamation, "Lord, if you had been here, my brother would not have died. But I know that even now God will give you whatever you ask" (John 11:20–21).

Her words revealed the struggle going on inside her. She did not demand that Jesus bring her brother back to life. Instead, she expressed what she believed Jesus *could* do without defining what she thought He *should* do.

Jesus dealt with the grief of the sisters by gently leading them into deeper intimacy with Him. To Martha He uttered these astonishing words: "I am the resurrection and the life. He who believes in me will live, even though he dies; and whoever lives and believes in me will never die. Do you believe this?" (John 11:25–26).

Martha's response, considering the circumstances, was also astonishing: "Yes, Lord, I believe that you are the Christ, the Son of God, who was to come into the world" (John 11:27). This proclamation of faith would determine Martha's reaction to future circumstances and enable her to serve Him with contentment and joy.

Jesus confronts each of us with the same question: "Do you believe this?" When I stood beside my son's casket and cried, "Lord, if you had been there on that highway, my son would not have died!" a similar set of words echoed through my pounding head: "Sharon, I was there. I am the resurrection and the life. Mark is not dead. He is alive with me. Do you believe this?"

My identity as a believer, a child of the King, determined my answer. But would my whispered "Yes" push me through my anguish to a place where God could use me as a physical demonstration of His faithfulness? Even the power to whisper "Yes!" came from intimacy with Christ.

> (Not in your own strength) for it is God who is all the while effectually at work in you—energizing and creating in you the power and desire—both to will and to work for His good pleasure and satisfaction and delight. (Philippians 2:13 Amplified)

Who Am I in Christ?

When Jesus invited Martha to enjoy intimacy with Him, He knew that future circumstances might disillusion her and tempt her to doubt His love. His previous exhortation prepared Martha to confront this doubt and reconcile it. As a result, by the time her brother died, her faithfulness was rooted in God's character, not in her circumstances or emotions. She was willing to love and serve Him even when He did not do what she wanted or expected Him to do.

Similarly, God's character in us frees us to reflect His love and faithfulness despite our circumstances. Understanding our identity as children of God motivates and energizes us to become His promise keepers as we offer courage, hope, and confidence based on who we are in Christ. The following are some ways in which Scripture describes those who are in Christ:

> The salt of the earth (Matthew 5:13)
> The light of the world (Matthew 5:14)
> Children of God (John 1:12)
> Christ's friends (John 15:15)
> Christ's witnesses (Acts 1:8)
> A new creation (2 Corinthians 5:17)
> Ministers of reconciliation (2 Corinthians 5:18–19)
> God's workmanship (Ephesians 2:10)

Because of who our Father is, and because of the riches of our inheritance, we always have something to offer to others. The woman with physical disabilities can know she is not limited in her ability to serve God. The wife who grieves every month when her body tells her she is not pregnant can choose to display God's character in her sorrow because her identity is in being His maidservant, not in being a mother. A Christian widow can know that her life does not end when her husband's does because she can learn new ways of responding to her redemption. The woman who loses her job can work through her options with confidence because she knows that wherever God places her is her own specially assigned mission field.

Each of us can offer scriptural encouragement from the wellspring of the comfort God gives to us.

I cannot write these words without hearing the protests from women with broken hearts as well as the whispers from my own heart, "Sharon, this is so hard and these words make it sound so easy."

I share the anguish and struggle. Every morning when I awake, I express the same protests as I reread the headline in my soul: "Mark is gone." But God's indwelling Spirit gives me supernatural power moment by moment to choose submission to God, to reflect my identity as His child, and to seek His kingdom and His righteousness through obedience (Matthew 6:33).

I am learning that tearful disappointments do not mean God is absent but that He is walking in the fire with me. The future may change how I wait on Him, but it cannot change who He is, how much He loves me, or my calling to serve Him. Please listen to my words; they are still hot from the refiner's fire: *Circumstances do not change who you are. Your primary calling is to reflect the character and nature of God. Whether you are experiencing pain or prosperity, you have many treasures to offer people. When God calls you to offer the treasures of your inheritance, you are on holy ground. He is doing "soul work" and He is giving you the privilege of fulfilling His promises in a needy heart. This is grace.*

Getting Focused

1 Describe who you are.

Staying Focused

Day One

1 Are you a child of God? How do you know? (Read 1 John 3:1–3.)

2 Someone has said, "The truest thing about you is what God says about you." If you are God's child, what does He say about you? (Read Psalm 139:13–18; Romans 8:1–2; Jeremiah 29:11.)

3 How does God's view of you differ from your view of yourself?

4 Whose view is correct? (Read Matthew 7:24–27; Matthew 24:35; 1 Peter 1:24–25.)

5 Review your answer to "Describe who you are" in the Getting Focused section. Did you define yourself by what you do? If so, try again.

6 Review your answer to the previous question and write a prayer thanking God for the gift of your inheritance.

Day Two

1 Initially Martha defined intimacy with the Master by the way she viewed herself, a traditional Jewish woman. Why is it dangerous to define our value by our roles? Are your measuring sticks addressed in the following Scriptures? (Read Matthew 6:19–21; James 2:2–9; 1 Samuel 16:7; 2 Corinthians 10:12.)

2 Ask God to make you aware of every time that you determine your value by your own standards rather than His. Choose to obey Philippians 4:8–9.

Day Three

1 If you are God's child, you are "in Christ." According to the following Scriptures, what does it mean to be "in Christ"? (Read Romans 8:1; Ephesians 1:1–14.) Make a list.

2 Do you believe this? Write a prayer thanking God for each blessing on your list.

Day Four

1 Why is a growing understanding of our position in Christ important in the practice of encouragement? (Read Galatians 6:2; John 13:34–35; Romans 12:1–2.)

2 How has Christ loved you? Be specific. What will you do today to reflect Christ's love? Ask God to give you specific direction for interacting with at least one person. Refer to your answers to Day Three, #1.

Day Five

1 What is the "law of Christ" in Galatians 6:2?

2 How do we fulfill the law of Christ? (Read Galatians 6:2; John 13:34–35; Romans 12:1–2.)

3 God wants you to respond to His love by loving the same way. He wants you to be His serving hands, hugging arms, and praying heart. How will you keep the law of Christ today by loving another person in the way that God has loved you? Write the name of the person and describe what you will do to reflect Christ's love. Ask God to use your actions to keep His promises to that person.

Day Six

1 Review Philippians 2:13. Ask God to use His Word to stir up your passion for Him.

2 Respond to redemption with joy and ask God to make the ministry of encouragement your pattern for living. Whom will you encourage today? Be specific. Now do it!

Living Focused

Take some prestamped postcards to church this Sunday. Ask God to bring to mind the names of people He wants you to encourage. Write their names on the postcards. Pray specifically for them this week and send them the card telling them of your burden to pray. Remind them of one aspect of the joy of being "in Christ."

Chapter Three

DEBORAH, GOD'S PROMISE KEEPER

Ginny's Story

When sudden, agonizing pain put me flat on my back, the thought of all my responsibilities, especially that of caring for my active four-year-old son, Beau, caused me to panic.

I prayed for God's speedy healing and attempted to entertain Beau while anxiously awaiting some relief. About twenty minutes later, my friend Mary Beth stopped by for no special reason and saw that I was hurting. She offered some medical advice (she is a nurse), cheered me with her upbeat manner, and took away my heating pad and replaced it with a bag of ice. Then she dressed Beau, lured him to lunch, and took him for a walk in the park.

Then my friend Carol called. Upon hearing that I was flat on my back, she insisted on coming over to give me a therapeutic massage. After forty-five minutes of her treatment, the pain diminished considerably.

Mary Beth and Beau returned with lunch from a gourmet cafeteria, and when Mary Beth left, she took Beau with her. Another dear friend delivered a few groceries, left, and later came back with a complete dinner for my family.

When Mary Beth returned that evening with Beau, she bathed him, dressed him in pajamas, and put him to bed.

I did not contact any of these people. Was it a coincidence that they appeared? I don't believe so. I believe a gracious, loving God sent each one, and I'm thankful they responded to His prodding. Their simple acts of love spurred me on to give the same gifts of love to others.

The greatest encouragement I receive is from those who thank me. Sometimes it is for making a meal, sending a note, or dropping off a little gift. Sometimes it is for something as simple as a kind word. When they tell me how these acts lifted their spirits, I am motivated to do such things more often. God uses their gratitude to confirm His presence and direction in my life.

As I listen to God's counsel on how and whom to encourage, He shows me new ways and new opportunities. The more carefully I listen, the more clearly I hear Him!

Encouragement Principle 3

Encouragement is contagious.

Advertisers know something that God wants His church to understand: *People need to belong*. Perhaps you have seen this commercial at Christmastime: Lightly falling snow swirls around the occupants of a horse-drawn carriage. In the distance, an old-fashioned farmhouse with windows aglow and smoke curling gently from the chimney promises a warm welcome to the approaching, happy family.

The tears forming in my eyes prove to me that the advertisers have achieved their goal. They have connected with my need to belong. By causing me to think that their product will create in me that warm and welcome feeling whenever I use it, they hope to get me to buy it.

Often I hear lonely young women speak of their yearning for a friend they can depend on. Jesus addressed that yearning when He spoke of our need to love and encourage one another within the structure of the local church. My heart hurts when these women say, "I've tried to make friends in the church. I just don't know how to break through the barriers."

In the once-popular television series "Little House on the Prairie," the Ingalls family was connected to all the other families in the town. The conflict in nearly every episode revolved around a relationship and was resolved through relationships. The show was popular because it touched the universal yearning people have for a satisfying form of community life.

In contrast to the era of the Ingalls family, our society is fragmented by selfishness. "What's good for me" has become the determining factor in many decisions. Integrity, loyalty, and commitment are valuable only when they serve self-interests. Opinion shapes our beliefs about truth, and we let circumstances determine our morality.

In business, what's good for the "bottom line" determines decisions, and we give little regard to the effect these decisions will have on families and individuals. In families, we want to make sure our children have every opportunity for success, so we fill every minute with activities. And in our individual lives we rationalize immoral behavior by saying, "God wants me happy. This makes me happy. Therefore, it must be okay."

Feelings of self-fulfillment have replaced Scripture as the authority for the way we behave.

Even when our lives are filled with wholesome activities, we have a sense that something better is missing. Yet when an opportunity arises to help a person experiencing unexpected pain or difficult circumstances, we consider it more of an interruption than an opportunity.

Battered, emotionally scarred, and lonely people sometimes look to the church for solutions, only to find the same fragmentation there. Busyness, independence, caution, and self-defined morality permeate many congregations. Instead of finding open arms that will bind up wounds suffered in a self-centered world, hurting people find a closed circle that politely ignores them because they do not fit the prescribed image.

The Power of One Woman's Encouragement

The need for an encourager to arise amid a desperate situation is not new. In Judges 4, we meet Deborah, a woman whom God used to perform that task for the nation of Israel.

> Deborah, a prophetess, the wife of Lappidoth, was leading Israel at that time. She held court under the Palm of Deborah between Ramah and Bethel in the hill country of Ephraim, and the Israelites came to her to have their disputes decided. (vv. 4–5)

Deborah's passion for God made her available to Him and accessible to the people of Israel. According to Deborah's own words, "Village life in Israel ceased, ceased until I, Deborah, arose, arose a mother in Israel" (Judges 5:7).

Deborah's obedience infused with the power of God's Spirit enabled her to lead the Israelites out of bondage. Although God may not call any of us to a position of national leadership, He does exhort each of us to take new life to our own villages.

This is not as difficult as you may think. Consider *Merriam Webster's* definition of village: "a settlement usually larger than a hamlet and smaller than a town." Now consider your circle of influence. In most villages, a large country house is at the center. Consider yourself that country house and realize that God is not asking you to encourage the whole world—just your part of it.

Kathryn felt lonely and isolated when she suffered a miscarriage shortly after moving to a new town. She smiled through her tears as she described the women in her new church who immediately sensed her need to be connected and reached out in compassion to encourage her. Consider how dry and brittle her soul might have become if the spiritual mothers around her had not ministered to her.

Deborah's Story

Deborah came to prominence during a low period for the people of God. The book of Judges records the history of the Israelites—their roller-coaster rebellion against God and God's amazing forgiveness and long-suffering grace. In response to God's promise to drive their enemies out of the Promised Land (Deuteronomy 31:3), the Israelites eagerly committed themselves to serve God (Joshua 24:16–17, 21). Instead, they cycled downward into corruption.

God's instructions were clear: kill all the Canaanites—no peaceful coexistence with Baal worshipers, no intermarriages, no religious blending, no peace treaties (Deuteronomy 7:1–5; 20:16–18). But instead the Israelites chose to tolerate what God told them to destroy. Their disobedience broke their fellowship with God and eventually, through intermarriage, diluted their identity as His people. Five times in Judges 1, we read that they did not drive out the Canaanites completely. They wanted to enjoy the depraved pleasures of Baal worship, which included temple prostitution, fertility rites, idolatry, homosexuality, human sacrifices, and drunken sexual orgies.

Is it any wonder that God's anger burned against them (Judges 2:11–13) when they turned their back on Him and embraced the most depraved religious system on earth? God handed them over to Jabin, King of Canaan, and Sisera, the commander of the army. The cruelty of Sisera over the next twenty years drove the Israelites to repent and caused them to cry out to God for help (Judges 4:2–3).

Faithful Where God Called Her

God responded to their pleas by raising up Deborah to lead them (Judges 4:4). Deborah is a prototype of women today who have a zeal for God. In her we see many examples of encouragement. Her love for God was a beacon in the darkness. Deborah's wisdom as a judge attracted people from all over. She acted as mediator in their disputes and listened when they told about the terror of Sisera. She heard reports of his war machine and of the hopelessness and apathy of the Israelites. Deborah's passion for God awakened her to the plight of her people, and God told her what to do about it.

Deborah used the word *arose* to describe her response to the call of God (Judges 5:7). It's the same word used in Isaiah 60:1: "Arise, shine, for your light has come and the glory of the Lord rises upon you." The Hebrew word is *qûm* (pronounced "koom"), and it can mean "build, carry out, confirm, endure, establish, fulfill, raise up, restore, support."[1]

Deborah rose up, and in so doing she raised up, established, restored, and supported the people in her village. That is the essence of encouragement! And that is what God calls each of us to do. He wants us to look around our villages, see the needs, and rise up—not in our own strength, not with random acts of kindness—but with purposeful actions in His name, trusting Him to accomplish His work of salvation and sanctification.

The Hebrew word translated *mother* in Judges 5:7, implies the "bond of the family." People often say that the mother is the heart of the home. My own mother-in-law often says wistfully that when her mother died, the heart went out of her family. Without the "gathering place" of home, brothers and sisters may lose their feelings of connectedness to one another.

Deborah understood the bonding power of a mother, and she used it spiritually as well as judicially. And that is what we need today—women who are not interested in earthly power, status, and position, but who are committed to living out the redemptive work of Christ; women who are willing to ask God to make them "the heart" of their communities.

In the Jewish culture of Deborah's day, it was unusual for a woman to be in a strategic leadership position. If the people of Israel were looking for a leader to get them out of bondage, would they have chosen Deborah? No. They would have chosen a man's man, a warrior. But God had other ideas. He chose to reveal His wisdom in an unexpected way—through a woman. Like Deborah, we too can "rise and shine" when we are called through the power of His Spirit.

---

1 Edward W. Goodrick and John R. Kohlenberger III, *The NIV Exhaustive Concordance* (Grand Rapids: Zondervan, 1990), 1603.

Spiritual Mothering at Its Best

According to author Susan Hunt, spiritual mothering takes place when . . .

> A woman possessing faith and spiritual maturity enters into a nurturing relationship with a younger woman in order to encourage and equip her to live for God's glory.[2]

There is no better platform for the practice of biblical encouragement than in the spiritual-mothering relationship.

In Deborah we have a picture of a woman spiritually mothering her entire nation for the purpose of displaying God's glory (Judges 5:7).

God's Plan for Deliverance

In answer to the cries of his children the Israelites, God revealed to Deborah a plan that would free them from their bondage. She told Barak,

> The Lord, the God of Israel, commands you: "Go, take with you ten thousand men of Naphtali and Zebulun and lead the way to Mount Tabor. I will lure Sisera, the commander of Jabin's army, with his chariots and his troops to the Kishon River and give him into your hands." (Judges 4:6–7)

Deborah challenged Barak with this command and strengthened him with God's promise of victory. Although Barak did not directly question Deborah's message, he agreed to go only on one condition: that Deborah go with him. Deborah did not command Barak to do something difficult and then leave him to fend for himself. She agreed to accompany him, which meant traveling about seventy miles with Barak and his troops back to Kedesh. Deborah's willingness to go along is evidence that the plan had

2 Susan Hunt, *Spiritual Mothering* (Franklin, Tenn.: Legacy Communications, 1992), 12.

come from God, not from her own imagination. She was willing to put her life at risk because she believed God and she believed the message He had given to her.

Deborah did not try to supplant Barak's authority. She acknowledged that he was the warrior and that it was his role to lead the men into battle. Her role as a prophetess was to inspire and encourage. Remember the definition of encouragement: "to give courage, spirit, or hope." The Holy Spirit prepared Deborah to be the encourager, but He did not equip her to lead an army into battle. God called Barak to perform that task. Deborah didn't try to be a one-woman show. She worked with others to accomplish God's victory, and that is precisely how the Body of Christ is to function today.

Dying to Self

Deborah's courageous response to Barak's request was contagious. Her bravery made the warriors willing to accompany Barak into battle. The words of Jesus in John 12:23–28 define the devotion exemplified in the Israelites as well as the lifestyle He calls believers to cultivate:

> The hour has come for the Son of Man to be glorified. I tell you the truth, unless a kernel of wheat falls to the ground and dies, it remains only a single seed. But if it dies, it produces many seeds. The man who loves his life will lose it, while the man who hates his life in this world will keep it for eternal life. Whoever serves me must follow me, and where I am, my servant also will be. My Father will honor the one who serves me. Now my heart is troubled, and what shall I say? "Father, save me from this hour"? No, it was for this very reason I came to this hour. Father, glorify your name!

Humans view death negatively, yet Jesus defines death as the way to life. He exhorts us to be "living sacrifices." This of course is impossible to accomplish in human strength alone. Living unselfishly requires the grace of God and the power of His Spirit.

Following a great hymn of praise describing the glory of God in Romans 11, Paul gives this exhortation:

> Therefore, I urge you, brothers, in view of God's mercy, to offer your bodies as living sacrifices, holy and pleasing to God—this is your spiritual act of worship. (Romans 12:1)

According to Colin Brown, "The sacrifices that remain for the Christian are those of praise and good living."[3]

Preparing a Bible study for a group of women requires a sacrifice of time, but God often converts those minutes and hours into a wealth of wisdom that multiplies goodness in the lives of those who attend as well as the one who teaches. It is a financial sacrifice for a mom or dad to cut back hours at work to spend time with a child, but doing so plants seeds of love in that child's heart that will be ready for harvest years later. Entering the crucible of suffering with a hurting friend requires a sacrifice of energy and emotion, but God can use it to heal a broken heart and deepen the encourager's understanding of God. Dying to self is a mysterious concept that goes against all natural instincts, but God promises to give us a new life if we willingly lay down our old one.

The fruit of Deborah's "living sacrifice" for God was forty years of peace (Judges 5:31). Her confidence in her identity as a woman belonging to almighty God empowered her to help people sort through confusion and darkness. The response of the men called to battle shows that within the ranks of Israel were people with embers of enthusiasm for God. They needed a leader to stir those embers into flames. Deborah—empowered by the Spirit, accessible to the Israelites, and available to God's call— was that leader. Her burning passion for God was contagious.

God confronted every Israelite, including Deborah, with the mandate to love the Lord their God with all their heart, soul, and strength (Deuteronomy 6:5). Deborah's life reveals that she believed God's promise of faithfulness to His people, that she loved

---

3 Colin Brown, ed., *The New International Dictionary of New Testament Theology*, vol. 3 (Grand Rapids: Zondervan, 1978), 434.

Him and would not bow to Baal, and that she did not relegate her allegiance to God to a specific day or hour. Her response to God's faithfulness was wholehearted obedience.

Today Jesus draws us with a similar command:

> A new command I give you: Love one another. As I have loved you, so you must love one another. By this all men will know that you are my disciples, if you love one another. (John 13:34–35)

The depth of our devotion to God will be revealed in us as it was in Deborah—in our relationships to others.

Deborah obeyed God's call because she understood that her position as His daughter compelled her to minister to her people. Her pathway to victory was not without conflict, however. Although many Israelites caught her vision for victory, others refused to join the battle.

Spiritual risk requires that we break out of the protective shell of "religious performance" and allow the seeds of encouragement to spill onto the fertile soil of other people's needs, where they will grow and bear fruit for years to come. Are you willing to crack the shell that makes it impossible for you to connect with others? Will those who live in your presence be drawn into the family of God because of the way His character is spilled out in your life?

Getting Focused

1. Consider the people in your circle of influence. What are the greatest needs?
2. Has anyone recently ministered to you without knowing it? Have you thanked the person? Doing so is a form of encouragement.

Staying Focused

Day One

1. God tells us that "faith comes by hearing and hearing by

the word of God." If we are to understand our position as "daughters of the King" we need a renewed commitment to hear His words, which will increase our faith. Allocate 20–30 minutes to read Psalm 119 and list the words describing the writer's passion for the Word of God.

2 Ask God to cultivate in your heart that same passion.

Day Two

1 Reread Psalm 119. List the results of the writer's reverence for God's Word.

Day Three

1 It is unlikely that God will call any of us to lead our country out of spiritual bondage, but He is calling us to shine in our personal "village." Who lives in your "village"?

2 List the people in your circle of influence (including those who require extra grace). If you asked them, what would they say is the driving force in your life? Find out!

3 Pray for each person in your circle of influence by name and ask God for an idea of how you can reflect the love of God to them.

4 Write a plan to build a bridge of encouragment to someone in your village. Begin today to carry it out.

Day Four

1 Read John 12:23–28. Review your bridge-building plan.

2 How often does your desire to do God's will conflict with your desire to do your own will?

3 What action is God requiring from you that will be difficult to perform?

4 In what ways will you have to "die" to obey Him?

5 Ask Him to equip you for the job and enable you to trust Him to bring your sacrifice to life.

Day Five

1 Reread Psalm 119:4–5. Although the psalmist is clearly passionate for God, he admits that he continues to struggle with obedience. Do not be surprised by feelings of inadequacy as you cultivate your relationship with God. The brighter His light shines, the more we see the need for change.

2 Reread Psalm 119:56–60. What steps does the writer take in developing his relationship to God?

Day Six

1 Deborah's obedience flowed from her commitment to God's truth. Using Psalm 119 as a guide, write a letter to God expressing your desire to revel in your position as His daughter and to delight in obeying His Word. For example,

Dear God, teach me to seek You with all my heart and thus understand my relationship to You (v. 2.) Shine the light of Your Word into the corners of my heart and show me when my ways and thoughts are unstable (vv. 5–6). Teach me the discipline of hiding Your Word in my heart so that I will not sin against You (v. 11). Teach me Your decrees (v. 12). O God, I want to rejoice in obedience and delight in Your decrees (v. 14). I will not neglect Your Word (v. 16). I will meditate on Your precepts and consider Your ways and rejoice anew in Your redemption (v. 15). Consume my soul with longing for You (v. 20) and open my eyes that I may see wonderful things in Your law (v. 18). Remind me that obedience sets my heart free (vv. 32, 60). Teach me the joy of instant obedience (v. 60). Turn my search for love into delight in You (vv. 35–37). I promise to meditate on Your Word so that I will grow to love you more, understand that You are good, and trust that what You do is good (v. 68). When it comes right down to the bottom line of life, all I have is your Word. It is more precious than thousands of pieces of silver and gold (v. 72). Please, I beg You, help me understand its depth and beauty (v. 27). I long for You. O God, keep my eyes fixed on You and Your redemption. Make my life flow from that source. Amen.

Living Focused

God equips us to offer the treasures of biblical encouragement when we immerse ourselves in His love. Consider creating a special place reserved just for your time with the Master. A comfortable chair in a corner, good lighting, a small table with favorite pictures of people in your "village," a healthy plant, extra pens, your journal, and a Bible. Fill a carafe with a favorite hot drink.

I hear your protests. No room, no time, too many interruptions. Really? Building strong village life starts with a deepening awareness of your position as a daughter of the King. Cultivating a passion for God requires sacrificial choices. Will you make them?

Chapter Four

TAKING RESPONSIBILITY FOR ONE ANOTHER

Sherry's Story

"Sherry makes the best chocolate chip cookies! If you're nice to her, shell give you a bag!"

The words of my friend reminded me of the reputation I had earned early in my marriage for giving small, brightly tied bags of homemade cookies to encourage or thank a friend.

Life was simple then. I enjoyed seeing people smile when they read my thank-you notes, and I worked hard to uphold my reputation as a "cookie" encourager. But after a few years, the joy faded. Eventually, I stopped making cookies, rationalizing that my life had become busy with more important things.

My acts of encouragement were so helpful at first. Why not now? Then I heard the voice of conviction: *Sherry! God is the encourager. You are only His vessel. When you seek His guidance, the Holy Spirit will direct your steps, and His love will flow through you*.

At the time I was very busy with struggles at church, so I didn't pay much attention. Our congregation was about to split and eventually did. Then, exhausted by our unsuccessful efforts to make things better, our family moved to another congregation. Hurt, disillusioned, and wondering how I could rekindle intimacy with God, I recalled my earlier encouragement ministry. Maybe I needed to pay attention when He prompted me to encourage others. After all, He promised to lead me.

Through profound tragedy He proved that His promise was true.

We met our new pastor and his wife through various dinner dates and church activities. Our friendship grew as we learned of our similar views and interests. My father was a minister, so I understood many good and not-so-good aspects of full-time Christian service.

Then a late night phone call threw our young friendship into a realm of darkness and uncertainty. As I heard the words accident and Mark, I braced myself for the list of his injuries. There was only silence, and my soul uttered a silent gasp. Our pastor's sixteen-year-old son and his girlfriend had been killed in the accident.

Oh, God, what do I do? Surely they need the comfort of their old friends rather than me.

As I went through the receiving line at the memorial service, Sharon greeted me. "What a way to begin a friendship!" she cried as we hugged. Then she whispered, "Just don't give up on us."

So many people streamed past her that day. Did she even realize what she was saying or to whom she was speaking? I was sure I couldn't give them the encouragement they needed. Besides, what would people think if this new kid on the block plowed into established circles? Old insecurities cried out, "Others will encourage them. You don't know them well enough to help. You'll say or do the wrong thing and make their pain worse. You don't know how they feel. You have enough other people in your life to worry about. They don't need you."

This time the voice of conviction spoke even more loudly. Sherry, God is the encourager. You are only His vessel. Follow the Holy Spirit's guidance.

I decided then that I would follow God's leading as He prompted me to minister in various ways to this family. For the first year I sent a card of comfort or encouragement once a week; during the second year I sent one once a month.

It has been exciting to see how God has used the right card, mailed on the right day, to minister to them. Sharon told me once that the card she received that day used the very same words she had used earlier to describe her sadness to her husband. The card reminded her that God knew what her thoughts would be before she even thought them.

How loved I feel to know that God loves people through me. I've learned that my early efforts to encourage people became a chore because I carried the load instead of letting God use me. Now I understand that I am not the only encourager He has and that He does not give me every burden to carry.

When I remain intimate with God, the Holy Spirit places suggestions in my mind. I've started baking cookies again, but now I pause and ask, "Lord, is this your idea or is it coming from a personal motive?" When I feel a sense of peace, I proceed. How privileged I am when He uses me to revive courage in the hearts of my friends.

Encouragement Principle 4

We revive village life when we take responsibility for one another.

A light of love pierced the tragic darkness in Kitwit, Zaire, when the deadly Ebola virus struck the inhabitants in 1995. About a dozen Red Cross volunteers, placing themselves at great risk of infection, carried numerous corpses from the hospital to their mass graves. Instead of applauding the selfless heroes, however, the townspeople treated these brave servants as pariahs. Fearing the disease, friends and neighbors avoided the volunteers. Storekeepers refused their money, believing it to be contaminated. The volunteers received six dollars per month, if available. Why did these Red Cross workers willingly place themselves and their families at risk? One volunteer stated, "It's a sacrifice, but it's a job that has a calling. It's a gift. We're exhausted, but we can't just let the situation go on." Speaking of these volunteers, one reporter said, "These are people of intense faith. They have a deep sense of community and duty."

What a profound picture of compassion flowing from a sense of community and faith!

When Isaac blessed Jacob, he proclaimed that God would make a community out of him:

> May God Almighty bless you and make you fruitful and increase your numbers until you become a community of peoples. (Genesis 28:3)

In Jeremiah 30:19–20, 22, we read God's promise to restore Israel from captivity:

> From them will come songs of thanksgiving and the sound of rejoicing. I will add to their numbers, and they will not be decreased; I will bring them honor, and they will not be disdained. Their children will be as in days of old, and their community will be established before me; I will punish all who oppress them. So you will be my people, and I will be your God.

God expected the nation of Israel to view themselves as a community separated from the world and connected to Him. Similarly, God calls the New Testament church a people separated from the world and connected to one another through their relationship to Him:

> But you are a chosen people, a royal priesthood, a holy nation, a people belonging to God, that you may declare the praises of him who called you out of darkness into his wonderful light. Once you were not a people, but now you are the people of God; once you had not received mercy, but now you have received mercy. Dear friends, I urge you, as aliens and strangers in the world, to abstain from sinful desires, which war against your soul. Live such good lives

> among the pagans that, though they accuse you of doing wrong, they may see your good deeds and glorify God on the day he visits us. (1 Peter 2:9–12)

Being part of a local church implies a spiritual connection rooted in common faith. The practice and demonstration of this faith is carried out not in isolation but in caring relationships. These relationships are at the same time dependent and interdependent. That is, people in proper relationship to God and others exercise leadership while practicing mutual submission and accountability. They express love by using diverse gifts for the common good. The church is a community of mutually dependent believers organized for a common purpose—to advance the kingdom of God.

The Israelites forgot their identity and purpose. Otherwise they would have responded willingly to the need when Deborah called them to arms. Sadly, some tribes refused to help.

The Need

God emphasized to the Israelites that their behavior must flow out of their relationship to Him (Joshua 23:10–11; 24:1–14; Deuteronomy 6:1–12). Just as Deborah's faithfulness to God flowed from her spiritual identity, the Israelites' disobedience flowed from the rejection of their identity as God's covenant people. This loss of identity caused community life to crumble because the people no longer recognized their common heritage or their common purpose. They lost their sense of mutual belonging and with it their sense of mutual responsibility. And once they no longer felt responsible for one another, they no longer saw the need to encourage one another.

Just as any healthy relationship requires good communication, so does a healthy community. Fear had disrupted Israel's communication system. Caravans ceased to travel because of unsafe highways (Judges 5:6). Those who had to travel took hidden routes to avoid molestation by their enemies. Agriculture failed as Israelites deserted unprotected villages and sought safety in the cities. But the cities offered no protection against forays of the Canaanites. Even the walled cities were under siege with the ravages of war at the gates. With an army deprived of its weapons and reduced to about 40,000 men (Judges 5:8; cf. 1 Samuel 13:22), Israel was ill-equipped for war. It would take a miracle to turn their plight around.

And that is what God provided when Deborah responded in obedience to His call.

The victory song of Deborah praises the receptive hearts of the winning tribes, but it laments the reluctance of the tribes that did not respond (Judges 5:15–17).

The four and one-half tribes that refused involvement might have felt relief when they heard of the victory. Perhaps they considered their inaction godly since, as they saw it, they weren't really needed. However, Deborah saw their neglect as disobedience—a refusal to seize a divine opportunity to participate in God's plan. They lost the treasures that would have been theirs if they had encouraged their oppressed family members by answering their call for help.

The responses of the various tribes of Israel illustrate the types of attitudes we find in the church today when there is a need for encouragement.

Asher—The Selfish Heart

The tribe of Asher illustrates the first reason believers refuse to practice biblical encouragement: *Our own lives are full of urgent demands*.

The tribe of Asher lived on the Phoenician coast. They refused the call to arms because of the demands of work on the ships and the docks (Judges 5:17).

Asher's narrow worldview kept them from seeing God's larger plan. They saw purpose in working for their own families, but they had no sense of being part of the larger body. They did not consider the needs of others a priority. Except for a brief involvement with Gideon, this tribe vanishes from the pages of Scripture.

Reuben—The Unsure Heart

The tribe of Reuben illustrates the second reason for noninvolvement: *We don't know what to do, so we do nothing!*

Reuben's tribe "searched their hearts" to consider what should be done. They could not overcome Sisera's iron chariots alone, but surely there was something they could contribute. Apparently they forgot that God's formula for victory often calls for the interaction of all parts of the body, each one contributing a piece of the solution.

God desires the whole body to be ministers of encouragement to one another. It is inappropriate to use private business as an excuse for neglecting public duty (Judges 5:15–16).

Reuben's tribe was sympathetic; they ached over the tyranny of Sisera. But they were not compassionate. Compassion involves action to alleviate the distress, whereas mere sympathy may remain detached and aloof.

Reuben's attitude is alive in many of us today. We feel sad when we hear about the needs of others. But, like Reuben, we're not sure what to do, so we stay within the safety and security of our own lives.

God calls us to action—not indecision—even if our action is imperfect. Choosing to do nothing grieves the Spirit. How often do we hurt others by our inaction? How many blessings do we miss due to our indecision?

What blessings would have accrued to this tribe if they had joined with other members of the family under the direction of the Holy Spirit? They had sympathetic hearts, but their sympathy did not drive them to express and demonstrate compassion.

Dan—The Stunted Heart

In the tribe of Dan we see the third reason for failing to become godly encouragers: *We give up when our initial efforts show no results.* Involvement in the lives of others does not come naturally; most people prefer personal tranquility. We fear saying the wrong word. Instead of stretching ourselves to find ways to encourage, we dodge difficulty and tiptoe around unpleasant places.

The word *linger*, used in Judges 5:17 to describe Dan's lack of action, implies a paralyzing fear or shrinking back due to fear. The stunted heart of Dan kept the tribe from realizing its full potential. They really never grew up. This pattern of immaturity started when the Amorites forced them into mountain country (Judges 1:34–36). Dan's tribe left their God-given territory and moved far north. God commanded them to overthrow their enemies, but they ignored His command to move forward and instead found a spot where they felt secure. Fear paralyzed their hearts, and their faith did not grow. In Judges 18 we read that the tribe of Dan eventually slipped into apostasy.

Intimacy with God transforms a stunted, fearful heart into a growing heart. It enables us to connect with others through the supernatural power of the Holy Spirit rather than withdraw into a cocoon of fear. Our obedience affirms that when God commands us to do a task He also equips us to accomplish it. We understand that God overcomes fear through our faithful obedience.

Gilead—The Insensitive Heart

In the tribes of Gilead (Gad and the eastern half-tribe of Manasseh) we see the fourth reason for the absence of encouragement: *We are insensitive*.

Gad and Eastern Manasseh refused to cross the Jordan River to lend their support (Judges 5:17). Because of the distance separating them, it is unlikely that Deborah expected huge support from these tribes. However, she rebukes them for their lack of any contribution to the victory. Lack of fellowship with one another will produce lack of enthusiasm for God's work.

The tribes of Gilead had lost contact with their fellow Israelites. They were insensitive to the desperation of those living under Sisera. Because they had forgotten their roots, they felt no obligation to respond. In the years to come, their enemies would repeatedly overrun them.

Lack of connection desensitizes us to the needs of others. Consider, for example, the plight of missionaries who are forgotten by the church at home. It's difficult for a local church to feel true compassion for their needs because of the distance separating them. Or, consider the needs of someone with a long-term illness or personal crisis. He or she can quickly become isolated from the rest of the body. Although their immediate needs may be met, their deep spiritual needs are often neglected. In both examples, out of sight means out of mind. Whenever we are separated by barriers like distance or circumstances, we need to make deliberate efforts to stay connected.

The City of Meroz—The Unresponsive Heart

The City of Meroz illustrates the primary reason we fail to offer encouragement: *We do not understand our identity in Christ.*

Deborah cursed Meroz, a town in Naphtali (Judges 5:23), for their inactivity. Clearly, Deborah expected great things from its inhabitants. Perhaps this city was near the war zone and in a unique position "to help the Lord against the mighty" (Judges 5:23). However, the inhabitants of Meroz guarded their peace and tranquility, apparently feeling no responsibility for their oppressed brothers. They did not see themselves as a part of this community.

People who are capable of contributing to the solution but are unwilling to become involved may not understand the treasures God has for those who practice encouragement. But Deborah would not accept that as an excuse. The people of Meroz heard of the need, dismissed it, and were cursed.

God calls His people to resist evil. If we turn a deaf ear to injustice and oppression when we could be agents of deliverance through sacrifice and toil, we subject ourselves to the same curse as Meroz.

We will be judged by what we have left undone as much as by what we have done. Jesus said, "I tell you the truth, whatever you did not do for one of the least of these, you did not do for me" (Matthew 25:45).

The practice of encouragement is rooted in our sense of belonging to Christ. He is our model. He is the One Who sets captives free, gives sight to the blind, and relieves oppression.

Considerate Hearts

Five and one-half tribes responded to Deborah's request for help: Issachar, Zebulon, Naphtali, Benjamin, Ephraim, and Western Manasseh (Makir). Benjamin, Ephraim, and Western Manasseh volunteered even though their regions were not directly affected by the oppressors. Deborah made her abode among these tribes.

Issachar's men rushed into battle with Barak (Judges 5:15) while the risk-takers from Zebulon placed their lives on the line (Judges 5:18). Naphtali's warriors assumed the most dangerous position as they took up posts in the high places. It was against these two tribes that the tyranny of Sisera was most felt. These tribes were willing to take risks and resolve the conflict because they had the most at stake. (Judah and Simeon aren't mentioned because they were well to the south.)

Deborah envisioned their positive response as an act of worship in which they entered the crucible of suffering and became part of the solution.

They saw the threat of Sisera against their brothers and sisters as a threat against themselves. They were a community bent on the true demonstration of the greatest of all acts of compassion—a willingness to die to protect one another.

After the victory, Deborah called all the people to worship—worship that was to cross all class barriers. Those riding white donkeys (the ruling classes) and those traveling on foot (the poor) were to listen to the singers reciting the righteous acts of the Lord and the righteous acts of His warriors (Judges 5:10–11). The revival of village life resulted in a new sense of freedom and in the breakdown of barriers that once had separated people.

In Deborah's song, she acknowledged the contribution of the

rulers and princes (Judges 5:2–3, 9), but credited God with the victory (vv. 4–5). This is an example of true biblical encouragement. It acknowledges the importance of the human element, but recognizes that the ultimate outcome rests on God's involvement.

The Problem

What had happened to cause the other Israelites to lose their sense of identity in God and thus their responsibility for one another? I believe there are three factors that contributed to the problem.

1. *They were satisfied with the status quo.* The first generation of Israelites took pockets of the Promised Land as God had commanded, but left certain parts untouched. The second generation, living in relative comfort and contentment, felt no urgency to continue the conquest of the Promised Land. Despite God's clear command that they not live among the Canaanites, they did.

We face the same problem today when we are content with our walk and do not take the necessary steps to remain passionately connected with God. We rest on one or more of our spiritual laurels (e.g., heritage or tradition), and forget that God's blessings are new and exciting every day (Lamentations 3:22–24). We lose the joy of serving God as we lose our spiritual identity in Christ. We forget that there are still new lands to conquer, new problems to solve, and God's strength available.

2. *They were more concerned with their own comfort than with obedience to the One Who was the source of their comfort* (Deuteronomy 6:10–12). God exhorts us to renew our minds daily as to who we are in Him. We are slaves. We have no rights except those given by our Savior. Any blessings we receive flow from His heart of mercy. Our sonship is a gift, an act of grace and compassion. To focus on the gift and not the intention of the Giver is to live in spiritual quicksand.

How do we overcome this attitude of entitlement? By cultivating a spirit of worship and thanksgiving for every gift. Giving thanks is music to God's ears. Worship is for our benefit—a reminder of the source of our many blessings.

In her song (Judges 5), Deborah reminds the Israelites that the victory over Sisera was not a right but a blessing from God.

3. *They had secondhand convictions and experiences*. The Israelites had neglected God's Word, so they had no personal experience with Him; their knowledge of Him was based on the experiences of their forefathers, which made their faith impersonal and shallow. Although God's Word clearly commanded separation from the Canaanites, they disobeyed. Envy of the Canaanites fertilized the sin in their depraved hearts. Israel was controlled by the flow of opinions and impulses from Canaan, and their daily activities focused on their own comfort.

Israel's foreign policy reflected their domestic policies, and disobedience in small daily matters had made them unresponsive to God in matters of national crisis.

The Solution

How do we combat such neglect? By keeping our relationship to God alive and growing through the study and application of His Word. Knowledge is simply not enough. Obedience translates mere Bible knowledge into a vital relationship. We must learn to apply our knowledge in very practical ways. And the place to begin is in our circle of influence, among those to whom God has called us to minister.

In our relationship to God we must always cry out, "More about Jesus would I know. . . ." But this is not enough; we must also sing, "More of His grace to others show. . . ."

Our passion for God deepens when we understand that His love constrains us to be His ambassadors (2 Corinthians 5:20). As we practice the discipline of praise, we will be driven to minister to those who need to know about God's love.

Although enough warriors volunteered and the war was won, Deborah did not let the negligent ones off the hook. Even though she did not need more soldiers, their neglect was inexcusable. They needed to enter the battle not for the sake of victory, but for the sake of their own spiritual welfare.

We must ask ourselves some serious questions. Are there treasures of encouragement that we are withholding due to self-centeredness? God repeatedly exhorts us to selfless behavior that goes against our natural human inclinations.

One of the most successful techniques of Satan is to promote selfishness and relational conflict within the family of God. Consider his method of operation in Adam's family. Cain, jealous of his brother, Abel, killed him and then asked God, "Am I my brother's keeper?" And that is the question many of us are asking today. "Am I my sister's keeper?" God's answer has remained the same throughout the ages: Yes. "Love one another as I have loved you."

To overcome our self-centeredness God gives us a treasure map that is both ancient and new every morning. As we look into His eyes, we see the map that will guide us to the hidden treasure of our inheritance.

Hebrews 10 has the antidote to our lack of caring for one another:

1. *Come near to God* (Hebrews 10:19–22). God invites us to cultivate intimacy with Him through His Son, our Savior, the Lord Jesus Christ.

2. *Contemplate the redemption purchased by the blood of the Lamb* (Hebrews 10:23). His character, not our circumstances or emotions, is the basis for our hope.

3. *Connect with the family of God* (Hebrews 10:25). Listen as He prompts you to express compassion to members of your community.

4. *Consider the needs of the people in your village, whether believers or not* (Hebrews 10:24).

5. *Commit to acts of compassion that will alleviate distress and inspire courage, spirit, and hope* (Hebrews 10:24). As we answer His call to rise and shine, our lives will light up our homes and communities.

6. *Continue biblical encouragement* (Hebrews 10:25). Allow these words to move you from acts of selfishness to acts of service.

Getting Focused

1. Who lives in your village?
2. What disrupts your village life?
3. How do you revive your daily village life?

Staying Focused

As you ask God to teach you how to respond to your position in Christ, remember this:

> Not in your own strength for it is God who is all the while effectually at work in you—energizing and creating in you the power and desire—both to will and to work for His good pleasure and satisfaction and delight." (Philippians 2:13 Amplified)

God provides the power and desire—that's grace!

Day One

1. Read Judges 5. The way each of the tribes responded to Deborah's call revealed their concept of their identity as God's people. Do you see yourself in any of the following:

   Asher—The Selfish Heart
   Reuben—The Unsure Heart
   Dan—The Stunted Heart
   Gad and Manasseh—The Insensitive Heart
   City of Meroz—The Unresponsive Heart

2. If so, ask God's forgiveness and ask Him to cultivate your understanding of your identity in Him. Ask Him to break you out of that cocoon and for a specific way to connect. Most likely, He will start you with a small act. Obedience will teach you more about His grace and supernatural empowering. Now do it.

Day Two

1. Read Joshua 23:10–11, Joshua 24:1–14, Deuteronomy 6:1–12. How was God faithful to the Israelites? What are His expectations of them? How are they to serve?

> Because of the Lord's great love we are not consumed, for his compassions never fail. They are new every morning; great is your faithfulness. I say to myself, "The Lord is my portion; therefore I will wait for him." (Lamentations 3:22–24)

2. God promises to give us a new blessing every day. Start a "Blessing Book" and list all the blessings you experience. Acknowledge that they are from God, and ask God to make you aware of His actions in your life every day.

Day Three

1. Read 2 Corinthians 12:14. What is Paul asking for in his relationship to the Corinthians?
2. Read 2 Corinthians 8:1–7. What motivated the believers to give so abundantly?
3. Read Exodus 36:4–7. What is your motivation for serving? Has anyone asked you to stop serving or giving of yourself because you have more than met the need? Imagine the excitement if your church leadership announced, "Stop giving! You've given more than enough! We don't need any more money, nursery workers, or volunteers!" What was the motivation of the Israelites to give so much?
4. Continue adding to your Blessing Book. Thank God for each blessing.

Day Four

1. Read Romans 12:1–2. Paul urges the Roman believers to offer themselves as "living sacrifices." What does he say is their motivation to do such a thing?

2 What is a "living sacrifice"? How are our actions a "spiritual act of worship"?

3 What will you do today that will be a "living sacrifice"? As you obey God in this area, thank Him that your actions are a "spiritual act of worship" and that your intimacy with Him will grow because of your obedience. How will sacrificial living help you connect with someone else?

Day Five

1 Reread Romans 12:1–2. Paul states that if our minds are renewed, our behavior will change. Based on this statement of truth, why is it important to deepen your understanding of your identity in Christ?

2 What are some of the elements of your inheritance? List them in your Blessing Book. (For help, read Ephesians 1 and 2.) What will you do today to share with someone an element of your inheritance?

Day Six

1 Read Deuteronomy 29. Take note of verse 19. Village life ceased because the people forgot their identity as God's children. What is God warning against in this passage? Why is it dangerous to "ride the coattails" of another's spirituality? What will happen to "village life" when we do this?

2 Ask God to open your eyes to places where you are "resting on your spiritual laurels." Add to your Blessing Book the fact that God answered your prayer. What small act will you offer as a living sacrifice to the King of kings?

Day Seven–Bonus

1 Read 2 Corinthians 2:14–17. Paul states that as God, in His grace, equips us to triumph *in Christ,* He spreads everywhere the fragrance of the knowledge of Him. In

light of this profound truth, what opportunities do we have as children of the King and members of Christ's body?

2 Add this great verse to your Blessing Book!

Living Focused

Consider the reasons you neglect encouragement. Ask God to reveal to you someone you have neglected. Outline a plan to help carry the person's burden. Remember, God's plan may not be for you to remove the burden, but to help shoulder it. Now, do it!

Chapter Five

THE DIRECTING FORCE OF ENCOURAGEMENT

Kathy's Story

Within days after I trusted Christ as Savior, the Lord began giving me hope and courage through many sources. I asked Him for a friend, and He sent a woman who gave me a book that helped free me from a ten-year struggle with depression. He used a Christian speaker to point me to Romans 8:28: "And we know that in all things God works for the good of those who love him, who have been called according to his purpose."

Through believers who said the words I needed to hear or sang a song that spoke to my specific need, I began learning that God always keeps His promise to be faithful. Through books, I learned God's principles that set me free from patterns of sin in my life. And through God's Word, I learned about His love, mercy, and grace. For the first time I experienced unconditional love and found hope in knowing that He would never forsake me, despite my faults—past, present, and future. When I focused on His character and promises, I saw all the circumstances of my life in proper perspective.

God continues to encourage me through the teaching of my church, which uses His word to rebuke, heal, challenge, and draw me closer to Him. God does not cause me to suffer needlessly, but He uses my suffering to perfect His image in me. It is up to me to choose how to respond to life, so I ask for the strength to choose joy despite the circumstances.

God's work in my life is for a purpose. I now have a heart for those who suffer from rejection, depression, divorce, and the trials of single parenting. I want to encourage these precious people and show them that God is faithful and trustworthy. Where He guides He provides.

Encouragement Principle 5

The directing force behind encouragement is God's Word.

In the months following Mark's death, I rushed home from every errand, eagerly sorted mail, and anxiously listened to phone messages. When I asked myself, *Why are you so desperate for mail and phone calls?* I realized I was hoping someone—anyone—would relieve the unending ache in my heart. When the phone did not ring, cards did not come, and no one visited, my shattered heart begged for physical comfort.

On those days God helped me realize that He alone was my encourager. All of the encouragement I had received from the body were initiated by Him and came from Him. I knew, therefore, that He was sufficient even on the days when I had no physical evidence of God's presence.

The phone calls, cards, and visits were pinpoints of relief, but I still had to face the emptiness of each day without my youngest child. God knew that the resolution for me would be to embrace the truth of the message one friend sent: "There are some wounds only heaven can heal."

Through excruciating confusion and grief, I learned that the purpose of all encouragement is to point us to the satisfaction only God can give. Encouragement prompted by the Holy Spirit and based on Scripture drives us to intimacy with God, enables us to rise above the routines and crises of life, and results in His glory.

Encouragement Is a Process

Biblical encouragers know that their role is part of a process; it is seldom, if ever, the solution. They understand that God is doing soul work through the interaction of the members of His body. They recognize that He uses circumstances to strip people of obstacles that keep them from knowing Him, and so they ask themselves, *How can I help this person through the peeling process of sanctification without hindering what the Holy Spirit is doing?*

Often we want to rush into a difficult situation and make everything better. But that is not God's method. He uses the rough spots of life to sand away the rough spots in character so that the reflection of "Christ in us" becomes increasingly clear.

In the months following Mark's death, encouragement from the body of Christ kept me from drowning in sorrow. In time, however, I came to realize that the only way for me to stay afloat was to spend time in God's Word. I began spending hours searching Scripture, and God used His Word to buoy me while I learned to swim in my new and unfamiliar circumstances.

My time in God's Word also gave me messages of love and truth that I was able to use later to help keep other struggling people from going under when difficult circumstances were pulling them down.

God is the one who sanctifies. Our job is to participate with Him in the process—not as pain remedies but as pain relievers.

If, however, we respond purely on the basis of how we feel rather than on what we know, we will tend to look for ways to eliminate hurt rather than for ways to act as the arms and hands of God to uphold the hurting person while God accomplishes His purposes through the adversity.

For example, some parents seem to believe that their primary role is to insure that their children live lives free of all pain. Thus, whenever their children get into trouble, the parents remove the source of discomfort, forgetting that God's purpose may be to use the unpleasantness to teach them a valuable lesson about the natural consequences of certain types of behavior.

Contrast these parents with those who pray, "Lord, I hate to see my child hurting, but I know that she needs to learn to lean on You, not me. Show me how to come alongside her in this difficult moment, and show her the work you are doing in her life."

Encouragement Is Discerning

In his letter to the Philippians, the apostle Paul suggested that our ability to "discern what is best" depends on love that is grounded in knowledge and insight.

> And this is my prayer: that your love may abound more and more in knowledge and depth of insight, so that you may be able to discern what is best and may be pure and blameless until the day of Christ, filled with the fruit of righteousness that comes through Jesus Christ—to the glory and praise of God. (Philippians 1:9–11)

We would do well to pray the same prayer. Love based on feelings and emotions clouds our ability to discern God's purpose and direction. But love that is based on knowledge—knowledge of each other as well as knowledge of God—leads "to the glory and praise of God."

In the book of Acts, for instance, we read that Paul and Silas were praying and singing hymns to God even though they were in prison and had been severely beaten. This indicates that their faith in God did not depend on their circumstances; it was based on their knowledge of God and their belief in His sovereignty. They were, therefore, not afraid of what any earthly force could do to them—even a force as powerful as the Roman government of that time. Although to others it may have seemed as if God had abandoned Paul and Silas, the two of them knew better. Their belief in God dictated their response to their circumstances.

Likewise, when we embrace the doctrine of God's sovereignty, we will see His hand at work and be better equipped to offer encouragement. If, however, we refuse to spend time getting to know God, our ability to encourage others will be severely diminished in that it will be based on our own limited understanding of ourselves rather than on our understanding of God and on His unlimited understanding of us.

Relationships do not grow toward intimacy if one party refuses to get to know the other. God knows us totally, but that is only half the equation. We need to know Him as well, and He invites us to do so.

Encouragement Is Compassionate

Listen as Paul exhorts the Colossians to live as a compassionate community by letting the word of Christ "dwell" or "take up housekeeping" in them:

> Therefore, as God's chosen people, holy and dearly loved, clothe yourselves with compassion, kindness, humility, gentleness and patience. Bear with each other and forgive whatever grievances you may have against one another. Forgive as the Lord forgave you. And over all these virtues put on love, which binds them all together in perfect unity. Let the peace of Christ rule in your hearts, since as members of one body you were called to peace. And be thankful. Let the word of Christ dwell [take up housekeeping] in you richly as you teach and admonish one another with all wisdom, and as you sing psalms, hymns and spiritual songs with gratitude in your hearts to God. And whatever you do, whether in word or deed, do it all in the name of the Lord Jesus, giving thanks to God the Father through him. (Colossians 3:12–17)

When we turn to Scripture, we enter the presence of God. And that is where we learn to face the life He has for us. We cheat our fellow believers if we neglect God's Word, for how can we minister in the name of Jesus if we don't know the power of that name in our own hearts? It is only through the knowledge of His Word and the power of His Spirit that we can become His promise keepers.

Imagine yourself as a young mom with several lively children cooped up in the house due to rain. When the weatherman announces that sunshine is on its way, you pack the children and their friends into your car and hurry to the beach. On arriving, the children tumble out of the car and run toward the waves, leaving trails of discarded clothing in their wake. Off come the hats, shirts, shoes, and socks. With innocent abandon they celebrate their freedom by twirling around and around, arms and hands lifted toward the sun, laughing gleefully. You smile and wish you could express and experience the same joy and freedom.

God's Word tells us we can.

> I hold fast to your statutes, O Lord; do not let me be put to shame. I run in the path of your commands, for you have set my heart free. . . . I will walk about in freedom, for I have sought out your precepts. (Psalm 119:31–32, 45)

Obedience to His Word deepens our intimacy with Him and empowers us to be biblical encouragers—confident of our ability to minister in His power, but wise enough never to attempt doing it in our own.

Encouragement Is Good

Scriptural encouragement is ongoing, daily, and consistent. It includes the practices of strengthening, motivating, assuring, supporting, exhorting, and disciplining. Webster's dictionary defines encouragement: "To give courage, spirit, or hope; to stimulate."

Consider how God's Word satisfies this definition.

> All scripture is God-breathed and is useful for teaching, rebuking, correcting and training in righteousness, so that the man of God may be thoroughly equipped for every good work. (2 Timothy 3:16–17)

This passage promises that God's Word equips us for every good work that God calls us to do. Encouragement is one of those good works, and Scripture gives us confidence to step into circumstances that call for the good work of encouragement. (Note: The passages listed with the following situations are not to be used as biblical solutions to the problems mentioned; they are to give you confidence that biblical solutions do indeed exist. It is up to you to find them.)

You see no signs of healing in the long-term depression your friend is suffering. You know that God wants you to stay by her side, but balancing your other responsibilities with her demands is draining your energy.

God's Word promises strength:

> The law of the Lord is perfect, reviving the soul. (Psalm 19:7)

Your child admits that he doesn't know how to combat strong temptation in the school he attends. You're not sure how to counsel him and wonder if you should change schools.

God's Word promises wisdom:

> The statutes of the Lord are trustworthy, making wise the simple. (Psalm 19:7)

A friend is in trouble because of her own foolishness. Scripture is pretty clear as to what she needs to do, but you wonder if it is your business to tell her.

God's Word promises joy from obedience:

> The precepts of the Lord are right, giving joy to the heart. (Psalm 19:8)

Mixed emotions flood your heart as your neighbor and friend tearfully confesses her marital unfaithfulness. She exclaims that her life is a mess and she doesn't know where to turn.

God's Word brings hope:

> The commands of the Lord are radiant, giving light to the eyes. (Psalm 19:8)

When your children were small, you taught them to live by scriptural principles. Now they are pushing against the moral boundaries, claiming that you are old-fashioned and that "no one lives that way anymore." You are beginning to doubt your decisions.

God's Word is everlasting:

> The fear of the Lord is pure, enduring forever. The ordinances of the Lord are sure and altogether righteous. (Psalm 19:9)

Shattered by the unexpected death of her husband, your friend cries, "I can't live without him. How will I face each new day?" Feeling helpless because you fear you would respond similarly, you don't know what to say.

God's Word is comfort:

> Remember your word to your servant, for you have given me hope. My comfort in my suffering is this: Your promise preserves my life. (Psalm 119:49–50)

You discover that your co-worker, a fellow believer, is cheating your employer. You're terrified to confront her, but you pray that when you appeal to her from Scripture she will repent.

God's Word convicts and corrects:

> I have considered my ways and have turned my steps to your statutes. (Psalm 119:59)

The more we make Scripture our lifeline to God and our guidebook for encouragement, the more we will cherish our time in it. The writer of Psalm 119 describes God's Word as wonderful (v. 18), a delight (v. 35), a comfort (v. 50), and more precious than thousands of pieces of silver and gold (v. 72). Then in Psalm 19:10–11 we read:

> [The ordinances of the Lord] are more precious than gold, than much pure gold; they are sweeter than honey, than honey from the comb. By them is your servant warned; in keeping them there is great reward.

When I read these two passages early in my grief, it was like hearing God say to me, "If you want to know Me, know my Word and obey it. I am the Word. Only I can give you courage, hope, and confidence. Choose to believe My words."

Believing that God uses Scripture to encourage us in our circumstances and to equip us to encourage others, I viewed every Scripture offered to my family through cards, conversations, and sermons as a lifeline to God. I trusted that in them was life. I continue to trust that one day His Word will set my heart free and allow me to walk about in freedom because I have sought Him and found Him in His Word.

My friend, Pat, understands the power of integrating God's Word into her life.

One day at a women's Bible study, Pat testified as to how God had released her from the tentacles of fear. Prior to her conversion, fear had enslaved her. When her son was small, she was so afraid of infection that she wouldn't let anyone near him without putting on a doctor's mask. Her son didn't know what people looked like from the nose down until he was two years old.

That same evening I received an emergency phone call from her. Her daughter had been in a serious car accident, but Pat wasn't calling simply to report the news. She was calling to report that her victory over fear was indeed genuine.

She had come upon the crash involving her daughter "accidentally." Even though the car was mangled by the collision, Pat recognized it and realized immediately that it was unlikely her daughter had survived.

She soon learned, however, that her daughter had survived but was trapped in the wreckage. Pat praised God for her victory over fear. Rather than becoming hysterical, as the old Pat would have done, she was able to sit in the back seat of the mangled car, hold her daughter's hand, and pray with her during the forty-five minutes it took rescue workers to free her.

The words of Scripture she had memorized were exactly the ones her daughter needed for comfort at that moment. The soothing sounds of those passages flowed from her heart to her daughter's ears as the clanking, whirring, and buzzing sounds of power tools and wrenching metal echoed around them.

Was Jesus in that car with them? No one could convince them otherwise. Why are they so sure? Because Jesus is the Word.

During a particularly difficult period of ministry in one of our churches, I met regularly with a friend to pray for resolution of the conflict. One day the turmoil reached such a point that we knew only prayer could calm us. We did not know how to pray, so we read to one another psalms that spoke of the presence of the Lord in the midst of turmoil. A miracle took place. The words calmed our spirits, silenced our sobs, and made us absolutely certain of God's presence.

Later, when the conflict increased even more, I protested that I could not handle any more pressure. I did not trust the motives of those who I thought controlled our destiny. As my husband, Chuck, and I lay on the bed talking, the tension caused my heart to tighten with anger toward people with whom I had once experienced sweet fellowship. I knew God could not release me from this anger as long as I insisted on my solutions, but I didn't want to wait any longer. Why weren't those in charge as wise as I?

Chuck opened his Bible to encourage me with Scripture, but my frustration only increased. Why couldn't he just pay attention to me?

"Here," he said gently, pointing to Mark 4:35–41, "read this out loud." As I forced myself to read, tears rolled down my cheeks. Like the tears washing my face, Scripture cleansed my spirit of the anger and frustration.

> That day when evening came, he said to his disciples, "Let us go over to the other side." Leaving the crowd behind, they took him along, just as he was, in the boat. There were also other boats with him. A furious squall came up, and the waves broke over the boat, so that it was nearly swamped. Jesus was in the stern, sleeping on a cushion. The disciples woke him and said to him, "Teacher, don't you care if we drown?" He got up, rebuked the wind and said to the waves, "Quiet! Be still!" Then the wind died down and it was completely calm. He said to his disciples, "Why are you so afraid? Do you still have no faith?" They were terrified and asked each other, "Who is this? Even the wind and the waves obey him!"

I could get no further than verse 39. As I read the words "Quiet! Be still," it was as if Jesus was there in the room exhorting me. If even the wind and the waves obey Him, surely He could bring order into our lives. The people I thought were in control were not in charge at all. Jesus was.

Those few words broke the chains of anger and anxiety squeezing my heart.

The power of Scripture to direct our lives along paths of peace and righteousness has been proved in my own life and in the lives of many godly women I know.

My friend Isabel describes her need to start each day cultivating intimacy with Christ:

> The most beautiful time of day is each morning as the sun comes up, so this is when I pray and read God's Word. As a twice-widowed woman, I need encouragement to start my day. His Word lifts me up; it helps me focus on the day's activities and think about who I will meet and how I will

> respond. Psalm 5:3 says, "In the morning, O Lord, you hear my voice; in the morning I lay my requests before you and wait in expectation." God is my encourager and I can depend on Him.

Isabel has caught the vision! But, you may protest, "I've tried starting my day earlier, but my children always get up. Do I have to get up even earlier to be obedient?"

Remember, we want to develop a relationship with Christ, not some new set of rules to follow. The only way to find out what is best for you is to prayerfully consider your day, lay your need for time alone with God before Him, and wait in expectation for His guidance.

There is no one-size-fits-all answer, but here are the stories of some women who have found an answer that fits them and their families.

Debbie, a home schooling mother of five, says,

> I am teaching my children that time with Jesus is not a luxury that we fit into our lives, but a necessity that we sacrifice to obtain. I set the oven timer for my quiet times with Him and tell them that this is God's time. They know they must not disturb me until the bell rings. Just as I would not cancel a doctor's appointment without a good reason, I will not cancel this time with my Savior. I hope they are learning to practice the same disciplines.

Olga says,

> Since I am a working mother, my best time to pray for others is on my way to work in the morning. Being alone in the car gives me complete privacy with the Lord. I do some of my most fervent praying there. I can talk to the Lord without any interruptions from the children, my husband, or a ringing phone! Since I can't look at a prayer list while I am driving, I trust the Lord to bring to mind people's names and situations He wants me to pray about.

> I read my Bible and have devotions during my lunch hour, one of the few blocks of time I have all to myself. I have chosen to use it for my spiritual nourishment and growth. I could never have that kind of hour in my busy home.

Although written in 1689 to a busy Duchess, the words of François Fenelon are just as appropriate for busy women today who long to know God:

> You must learn, too, to make good use of chance moments: when waiting for someone, when going from place to place, or when in society where to be a good listener is all that is required;—at such times it is easy to lift the heart to God, and thereby gain fresh strength for further duties. The less time one has, the more carefully it should be managed. If you wait for free, convenient seasons in which to fulfil real duties, you run the risk of waiting forever; especially in such a life as yours. No, make use of all chance moments. . . . One moment will suffice to place yourself in God's presence to love and worship Him, to offer all you are doing or bearing, and to still all your heart's emotions at His feet.[1]

I keep a journal—an intimate record of my spiritual pilgrimage—to remind myself of God's faithfulness.

After Mark's death, our daughter, Heidi, and her fiance, Greg, approached us and said they were willing to put off their wedding if that would help us in our grief. We responded, "The only reason to delay is if you two are not ready for marriage. And we think you are ready."

Heidi's friends planned a beautiful surprise shower for her, and I wanted to encourage my daughter to be as happy as possible even though my own heart sobbed with longing to have Mark share in this time. On the day of the shower I wrote in my journal, "God,

---

1 François Fenelon, *Spiritual Letters to Women* (New Canaan, Conn.: Keats Publishing, 1980), 21–22.

please give me a message that will release me to enjoy this time and to encourage Heidi to do likewise."

As part of my devotional time every day, I read a chapter of Proverbs (there are thirty-one chapters, so I read through the book once a month). Chapter 25 was my scheduled passage for this particular day, so I turned to it and began reading. God answered my prayer that day in a startling way, and this is how I recorded it in my journal:

> Nothing moved me until I read verse 25. "Like cold water to a weary soul is good news from a distant land." Then I prayed, *Oh, Lord, how true! How good it would be to hear a message from heaven, a distant land. How satisfying to my parched soul the fresh cold water of that message would be. Mark is alive in the Promised Land! How good if I heard those words.* I turned to Genesis 45:25–28, as suggested by the commentary, and gasped as I read:
>
> "So they went up out of Egypt and came to their father Jacob in the land of Canaan. They told him, 'Joseph is still alive! In fact, he is ruler of all Egypt.' Jacob was stunned; he did not believe them. But when they told him everything Joseph had said to them, and when he saw the carts Joseph had sent to carry him back, the spirit of their father Jacob revived. And Israel said, 'I'm convinced! My son Joseph is still alive. I will go and see him before I die.'"
>
> *Oh dear Jesus, I am taking this as a message from You, not a coincidence. Like Jacob rejoicing to know his son, Joseph, is alive, you are reminding me that Mark is alive in a distant land, waiting for us to come home. I believe this and it refreshes my soul! Thank You for being so specific in Your loving communication with me. I will go to Heidi's shower and encourage her to freely enjoy Your blessings.*

I use my journal as a dialogue with God. I record how I feel, and I lay my needs before Him. He responds through His Word and devotional books, which sometimes address the very idea I have expressed in my journal. In this instance, God used my daily Bible reading and meditation to give me the comfort I had prayed for.

Are you enjoying intimacy with Christ? Is Scripture the directing force in your life?

Some of you are thinking, "I would look forward to my quiet times if they were as specific and exciting as the ones you've described."

I want to be honest. Although I spent time in Scripture before my son's accident, it was his death that drove me to diligently search Scripture for hope. God promises that when we seek Him, we will find Him. Seeking is an aggressive word and requires disciplined action. Any discipline is difficult to maintain through periods when there are no apparent results. Spiritual disciplines are no different. Every morning I make a deliberate choice to spend time with Jesus, even on days when the Word tastes dry and God seems distant. Those are the times I must choose to believe the promise of Jesus:

> But the Counselor, the Holy Spirit, whom the Father will send in my name, will teach you all things and will remind you of everything I have said to you. Peace I leave with you; my peace I give you. I do not give to you as the world gives. Do not let your hearts be troubled and do not be afraid. (John 14:26–27)

Jesus promised that the Holy Spirit will teach us everything we need to know to enable us to live in peace.

One vacation we enjoyed relaxing on floats in the ocean as gentle waves lapped the shore. The water was warm and the only annoyance was an occasional crab nibbling at our feet—no jelly fish, no strong undertow, no flies on the beach. What more could we ask?

But one day the ocean changed. The water sounded angry as it pounded the beach. This was a day for caution.

Even five-year-old Elizabeth knew that something was different. "I don't want to go in the boat alone," my niece informed her father. "The waves are too high. You hold me and I'll go with you."

Elizabeth knew that she couldn't handle the waves by herself. Her youthful instincts told her what most grownups forget: We can't make it through life alone; we need help.

My heart's cry is that each of us will trust our heavenly Father the way my niece trusts her daddy. How foolish of us to expect to survive the rough waves of adversity without His strong arms around us.

Getting Focused

1 What is the directing force in your life?

2 Read Psalm 119:1–16. What is the directing force in the psalmist's life? What words describe his passion?

Staying Focused

Day One

1 Read 2 Timothy 3:16–17. How does God equip us to obey Him? List four purposes of Scripture. In light of this truth, what should direct your relationships with others? What should direct your own life?

2 What specific area of your life needs teaching, rebuking, correcting, or training?

3 To remind you of the power in Scripture, memorize 2 Timothy 3:16–17.

Day Two

1 Do people ever disappoint you? Read 2 Timothy 4:16–18. Where do you normally seek encouragement? Where should you seek encouragement?

2 How will you allow God to encourage you today?

Day Three

1 Read Psalm 40:10. David promises to tell others of God's faithfulness. How would his testimony encourage the people?

2 Read your Blessing Book. Write a two-sentence testimony about one specific blessing and ask God to give you an opportunity today to encourage someone else with the story of God's faithfulness to you.

3 Review 2 Timothy 3:16–17.

Day Four

1 Remember why the Israelites lost their sense of identity:
1. They were satisfied with the status quo.
2. They were more concerned with their own comfort than with obedience to the One who was the source of their comfort.
3. They had second-hand convictions and experiences.

2 Ask God to reveal if you are guilty of any of these. If you are, confess your neglect and commit to change.

Day Five

1 Read Colossians 3:12–17. With what godly qualities should we be clothed? What binds these qualities together? What place does the Word of God have in our relationships to each other?

Day Six

1 Compare the richness of a person's life when God's Word takes up housekeeping (described in Colossians 3:12 –17) to that of one who chooses to live according to his or her own wisdom.

2 Where do you go for wisdom regarding your relationships? Where will you go from now on?

Living Focused

If you have never kept a journal, start today. Record your thoughts, questions, and struggles. You don't have to be a writer, use good grammar, or spell correctly. This is between you and your Lord. Write out your prayers and note which Scripture passages God uses to direct your life. Include meaningful quotes. Your journal is a record of your spiritual journey.

Part 2

Living Biblically

Chapter Six

TREASURES IN THE CHURCH

Olga's Story

A newcomer to our church, whom people considered somewhat odd, told me one day how lonely she was in our church. Like most others, I had avoided her as often as I could, so I wasn't surprised to learn how she felt. Out of guilt, I took her under my wing. I invited her to family dinners, and we talked on the phone. I asked her to go with me to many of the women's functions at church, and I involved her in as many activities as I could.

To my surprise, the result was a mutual, loving friendship. She became like a sister to me. One day she told me a story that explained why she was "different."

Before moving to our state she had suffered brain damage in a car accident, and she had had to relearn many skills and abilities. In her previous church she had sung in the choir, but she had lost her ability to read music and was afraid to try again. Since our choir desperately needed altos, I nagged her for weeks until she joined. I figured a lousy alto was better than no alto. I knew the Lord would understand (and I prayed that the choir director would also).

We were all pleased to find out that she had a lovely voice, and it was a joy for me to sing with her. The choir director even gave her a solo part in the Christmas cantata.

My friend was a florist by trade and offered to make the prom bouquet for my son's date. She had not arranged any flowers since her accident, so it was with fear and trepidation that I consented. But my concern was unnecessary. The bouquet was lovely, and she is now preparing floral arrangements for church members' weddings.

Because our church gave my friend the opportunity to express her giftedness in a time of weakness, her confidence returned and she became a leader in our church. A few months ago, she wrote me a letter announcing that she is now the church nursery coordinator and missionary-fellowship organizer.

By reaching out to our "odd" newcomer, I was blessed, and so was the entire congregation. I saw God's plan for her (at least in part) unfold in front of me, and I still marvel.

Barbara's Story

At a spring retreat, women from our church studied how to minister in periods of profound loss. Two short months later we had an opportunity to put into practice the lessons we had learned.

A dear friend was visiting us to celebrate with our family the arrival of our much-longed-for baby boy. My friend had prayed with me through a long stretch of miscarriages and infertility problems while I had celebrated with her the births of her two beautiful children. What a precious time we shared.

But anguish interrupted our special celebration when her three-year-old daughter drowned in our backyard pool.

The retreat I had attended a few months earlier had equipped me to minister to my friend, and it had equipped the women in my church to minister to me. They became Christ's loving arms reaching out to comfort me. They faced the loss with me, and they assured me of Christ's presence in the darkness.

Programs are easily forgotten, but women who prayerfully put into practice what they learn at those programs are not.

Encouragement Principle 6

Biblical encouragement creates a loving community that causes others to glorify God.

First Peter 2:9-15 reveals one of the purposes God has for the local church:

> But you are a chosen people, a royal priesthood, a holy nation, a people belonging to God, that you may declare the praises of him who called you out of darkness into his wonderful light. Once you were not a people, but now you are the people of God; once you had not received mercy, but now you have received mercy. Dear friends, I urge you, as aliens and strangers in the world, to abstain from sinful desires, which war against your soul. *Live such good lives among the pagans that, though they accuse you of doing wrong, they may see your good deeds and glorify* God *on the day he visits us*. Submit yourselves for the Lord's sake to every authority instituted among men: whether to the king, as the supreme authority, or to governors, who are sent by him to punish those who do wrong and to commend those who do right. For it is God's will that by doing good you should silence the ignorant talk of foolish men. (Emphasis added)

God's plan for members of His church is to do good so that unbelievers will see God in us. When we view our lives as part of God's revelation to the world, our activities take on new meaning. God is revealing Himself through us, His body, the church. Consider the impact of evaluating all church activities in light of this purpose. A church focused on revealing God to the world will be known for one thing above all: love.

> Whoever does not love does not know God, because God is love. . . . And so we know and rely on the love God has for us. God is love. Whoever lives in love lives in God, and God in him. (1 John 4:8, 16)

In chapter 4 we studied an Old Testament example of community life being broken down. In the New Testament we have an example of community life being built up.

The Church at Philippi

Acts 16 records the beginning of the church at Philippi:

> During the night Paul had a vision of a man of Macedonia standing and begging him, "Come over to Macedonia and help us." After Paul had seen the vision, we got ready at once to leave for Macedonia, concluding that God had called us to preach the gospel to them. (Acts 16:9–10)

This dream changed the course of history. Instead of heading east, as they had planned, Paul and his colleagues headed west. Thus, Europe and the Western world were the first to hear the gospel, and that is why to this day Christianity is more prevalent in the West.

The first convert in Europe was Lydia, a businesswoman from Thyatira who lived in Philippi. Lydia worshipped God, but she did not know the Savior until her encounter with Paul. After her conversation with him, "The Lord opened her heart to respond to Paul's message" (Acts 16:14). Paul's obedience to the work God called him to do—spread the good news—allowed God the opportunity to do the work that only He can do—open people's hearts.

The Philippian church illustrates seven traits of an encouraging church.

1. Renewed Hearts

Paul and Lydia both illustrate that the Lord uses our lives after He has renewed our hearts. Shortly after his conversion, Paul (who was still called Saul) "spent several days with the disciples in Damascus" (Acts 9:19). Then, in a dramatic turnaround, he who so recently had been "breathing out murderous threats against the Lord's disciples" (9:1) became one of them himself and "at once . . . began to preach in the synagogues that Jesus is the son of God" (9:20). Lydia, likewise, responded immediately to God's work of renewal in her heart. As soon as the Lord opened her heart, "she and the members of her household were baptized" (16:15). A sure sign of a renewed heart is the willingness to identify with other believers. Paul expressed that willingness when he preached about Jesus in the synagogue, and Lydia expressed it when she was baptized.

We encourage one another when we make known to others the work God is doing in our hearts and lives.

2. Submitted Hearts

Believers are part of one body—Christ's—so whenever we are selfish, proud, disagreeable, or uncooperative, we ultimately harm the whole body. On the other hand, when we submit ourselves to others, putting their needs before our own, as Paul instructed the Philippian church to do, we encourage others to do the same.

> Make my joy complete by being like-minded, having the same love, being one in spirit and purpose. Do nothing out of selfish ambition or vain conceit, but in humility consider others better than yourselves. Each of you should look not only to your own interests, but also to the interests of others. (Philippians 2:2–4).

We encourage one another when we put the needs of others ahead of our own.

3. Connected Hearts

Immediately upon conversion, Lydia saw herself as part of a larger picture and identified herself as a believer in Christ.

> When she and the members of her household were baptized, she invited us to her home. "If you consider me a believer in the Lord," she said, "come and stay at my house." And she persuaded us. (Acts 16:15)

The first church in all of Europe started in Lydia's home because she recognized the importance of spending time with other believers.

We encourage one another when we spend time together.

4. Risk-taking Hearts

Lydia did not merely sympathize with the needs of Paul, Timothy, Luke, and Silas; she insisted on meeting them. She invited the four men to stay in her home while they went about their work. This was not a small favor she was offering. Acts 16:16–18 tells about a slave girl who followed them for "many days," which implies that Lydia had house guests for quite a long period of time. Lydia took the risk of asking four men she hardly knew to stay in her home for an indefinite period of time. As a result of their work and Lydia's willingness to take a risk, the church grew.

We encourage one another when we do the work of the Lord without worrying about personal inconvenience.

5. Generous Hearts

The practice of biblical encouragement within the local church equips us to meet the needs of the universal church. In Philippians, Paul commended the people for their generous support.

> I thank my God every time I remember you. In all my prayers for all of you, I always pray with joy because of your partnership in the gospel from the first day until now. (Philippians 1:3–4)

> Yet it is good of you to share in my troubles. Moreover, as you Philippians know, in the early days of your acquaintance with the gospel, when I set out from Macedonia, not one church shared with me in the matter of giving and

> receiving, except you only; for even when I was in Thessalonica, you sent me aid again and again when I was in need. (Philippians 4:14–16)

Lydia set an example of generosity when she opened her home to the church, and the Philippians followed it by financially supporting Paul's mission work. If your church has financial pressures that make it difficult to support missionaries, follow the example of the church at Philippi, which was one of the Macedonian churches Paul commended in 2 Corinthians 8:1–5:

> And now, brothers, we want you to know about the grace that God has given the Macedonian churches. Out of the most severe trial, their overflowing joy and their extreme poverty welled up in rich generosity. For I testify that they gave as much as they were able, and even beyond their ability. Entirely on their own, they urgently pleaded with us for the privilege of sharing in this service to the saints. And they did not do as we expected, *but they gave themselves first to the Lord and then to us in keeping with God's will.* (Emphasis added)

The Philippians saw the bigger picture, not just their own little part of it. Their giving was not reluctant but wholehearted. They did not dismiss the cry for help with lame excuses such as "We need to take care of our own. We can't even think about sending them money. Someone should be helping us."

By refusing to give in to their own selfishness, they helped spread the gospel of Christ's kingdom. Why? Because "they gave themselves first to the Lord and then to us in keeping with God's will."

We encourage one another when we give ourselves first to the Lord.

6. Accepting Hearts

Acts 16 mentions two of the new converts in the Philippian church: the slave girl who earned money for her owners by fortune-telling, and the jailer who guarded Paul and Silas after their arrest for casting an evil spirit out of the slave girl.

These probably were not the type of people Lydia was accustomed to associating with. Nevertheless, we can assume that she welcomed them into her home as part of her new spiritual family.

A church practicing biblical encouragement accepts broken people, knowing that each part is necessary to bring honor and glory to the body of Christ:

> It takes all God's ransomed children to make one ransomed child complete. A brick may have the appearance of a finished product, but it will still look rather forlorn until it is given its proper place in row and tier and all the rows and tiers are in, and the beautiful temple is finished. So also God's children, like so many living stones, will form a finished temple when Jesus returns, not until then. Believers are like the dawning light that shines brighter and brighter unto the coming of the perfect day, for it is then that he who began a good work in them will have completed it.[1]

When I asked friends what they liked about their church, many mentioned acceptance. One woman described her church as a place where "acceptance and love promote growth." Another said, "My church is a place where I can be vulnerable without fear of rejection or unkind criticism."

Fundamental to Paul's teaching is the message he sent to the Roman church:

> May the God who gives endurance and encouragement give you a spirit of unity among yourselves as you follow Christ Jesus, so that with one heart and mouth you may glorify the God and Father of our Lord Jesus Christ. *Accept one another, then, just as Christ accepted you, in order to bring praise to God.* (Romans 15:5–7, emphasis added)

1 William Hendriksen, *Philippians, Colossians, Philemon*, New Testament Commentary (Grand Rapids: Baker, 1962), 56.

In raising our four children, we learned quickly that they were not perfect. Although my husband and I were not happy when they failed, we were not surprised or distraught either. They were members of the human race, which earned them the right to the label "totally depraved." Our job as parents was not to sit back and enjoy the glory of their perfection, but to work to limit the effects of their imperfection through nurture, training, and discipline. Home was a place where they could learn from their mistakes in a loving, correcting atmosphere and find out how to live lives pleasing to God.

The church, like a home, is not a place where perfect people enjoy each other's company. It's a place where spiritual nurture, training, and discipline help imperfect people take on the image of their perfect heavenly Father. The church is not a place for hibernation; it's a place where we learn, grow, take risks, make mistakes, and get up and try again.

A church that practices biblical encouragement is not surprised by "people" failures, and it does not waste time and energy wondering, *How could he have done such an awful thing?* or *Why did God allow this?* It simply goes about the work of restoring people to fellowship with God and others (see Galatians 6:1).

My friend Barbara Thompson calls this process "moving women from misery to ministry." Our purpose is not to make people feel good about themselves, but to enable them to behave well for God.

We encourage one another when we welcome imperfect people.

7. Faithful Hearts

About ten years after the establishment of the church, Paul reminded the believers of the early training they had received and urged them to stand firm:

> For it has been granted to you on behalf of Christ not only to believe on him, but also to suffer for him, since you are going through the same struggle you saw I had, and now hear that I still have. (Philippians 1:29–30)

His words took them back to the period when they learned by observing Paul's life how to hold out the word of truth in the face of adversity.

The apostle John commended his friend Gaius with these words:

> Dear friend, you are faithful in what you are doing for the brothers, even though they are strangers to you. They have told the church about your love. You will do well to send them on their way in a manner worthy of God. It was for the sake of the Name that they went out, receiving no help from the pagans. We ought therefore to show hospitality to such men so that we may work together for the truth. (3 John 5–8)

He could have written the same words about the church at Philippi. Would anyone write them about your church?

We spread the seeds of the gospel every time we practice biblical encouragement in any form. When we work in the nursery, clean church toilets, empty overflowing trash cans, or wipe up excess water around restroom sinks, we are helping to spread the gospel through biblical encouragement.

Sunday school teachers plant seeds without knowing if or when they will sprout. They may lie dormant for many years before suddenly taking root.

In my journey through grief, I pleaded with God to let me experience His joy again. But I did not believe it was possible. Then I remembered an older gentleman who had taught vacation Bible school when I was a teenager. The text for our week-long Bible study had been Paul's letter to the Philippians. I remember very little about the study except the theme: joy, which our teacher delighted in reminding us.

In my search for joy many years later, God used that tiny seed to point me to Philippians. I have forgotten the man's name, but I pray that one day in heaven I will have the privilege of telling him how his faithfulness to a horde of ungrateful teenagers helped one of them survive the deepest sorrow of her life. This faithful man has a part in any spread of the gospel that God accomplishes through my life.

We encourage one another when we faithfully spread the gospel even when we don't see any results.

Consider the community of your local church. Are the hearts of believers in your community renewed? submitted? connected? risk-taking? generous? accepting? faithful?

If your answer is no, how might God use you to effect change? If your answer is yes, what are you doing to keep it that way?

Getting Focused

1 What are the first words you think of when you hear the word *church?*

2 Describe your church. Did you use the words *compassionate* or *community?*

3 Reread Olga's story at the beginning of this chapter. Do you have any Olgas in your congregation? Apply Psalm 68:6 to the situation: "God sets the lonely in families, he leads forth the prisoners with singing; but the rebellious live in a sun-scorched land." What opportunity for ministry might God be giving your local church family? Lydia widened the circle of her family to include new believers. Does your church family do the same? Do you?

Staying Focused

Day One

1 Read Philippians 1. Paul was in chains twenty-four hours a day, yet the theme of joy is evident. Define joy. Why did Paul have it? What gives you joy? Joy often comes when we reach out to another person. Who in your local church needs to feel more connected? List some ways you could connect with her. Some suggestions: Give her a ride to an event. Sit with her in church. Invite her to lunch. After doing this, encourage someone else by telling the story of what happened.

Day Two

1 Reread Philippians 1. Whom does Paul include in his prayers? Why was it important for him to say this to the Philippians? How does prayer build community? Look up the word *community* in the dictionary. What makes a group of people a community? What basic building blocks of community does Paul address in this chapter? With what group of people do you experience "community"? How will you build that community through the practice of prayer?

Day Three

1 Reread Philippians 1, this time noting specific themes. Read verses 9–11. Why did Paul pray that the love of the Philippians would grow more and more in knowledge and depth of insight? What are the dangers of emphasizing "love for Christ" with little regard for "right doctrine"? How does sound doctrine promote community? Is there a friend who would benefit from growing in knowledge? Invite her to a teaching program in your local church. Your invitation will promote community.

Day Four

1 Reread Philippians 1. How did Paul view his imprisonment (vv. 12–14)? Why did Paul rejoice (vv. 4, 18, 19, 25–26)? How does Paul's response to his imprisonment promote community? How will you promote community by your response to your circumstances?

Day Five

1 Reread Philippians 1. In verse 27, Paul exhorts the Philippians to "conduct yourselves in a manner worthy of the gospel of Christ." What is a "manner worthy of the gospel

of Christ" according to Ephesians 4:1–6? How does living in a manner worthy of the gospel cultivate community? Reread Olga's story at the beginning of this chapter. Is there an odd woman in your church who is lonely? How will you make her feel safe in your local church family?

Day Six

1 How did Lydia cultivate community (Acts 16:11–15, 40)? Paul often used the physical body as a metaphor to describe the body life of the church. For a body to work, every part must do its job. For the body of Christ to function properly, every part must live "in a manner worthy of the gospel." List three ways in which your life contributes to the community life of your local church.

Living Focused

Practice biblical encouragement this week by cultivating the compassionate community of your church. Tell a ministry leader that you are willing and available to obey God in whatever needs to be done—even if it involves the risk of inconvenience. Don't give up until you find someone who needs your help.

Chapter Seven

TREASURES IN CLAY POTS

Carolyn's Story

Shattered by several profound losses, I looked to my church as a safe place to heal. But the music of worship stirred the chords of my soul and brought to the surface my deep grief. Wanting to appear spiritually strong, I struggled not to cry, believing that tears were a sign that I had lost control. Heaven forbid that I should lose control in church! But my soul cried out, "If I can't weep in God's house with His saints to support me, where can I weep?" I decided then that tears were not shameful and that I would allow myself the emotional catharsis of weeping. During a service shortly after that, the music once again stripped away my façade of control and connected my broken heart to God's. This time I did not hold back the tears. A dear spiritual mother saw my body shaking with sobs and moved toward me.

Her willingness to step into my pain filled me with hope. Had I not allowed her to see my condition, however, I'm not sure she would have moved into my life. God continues to use her to bring healing to my life with prayers and words from Scripture, which always give me a new perspective from which to view my circumstances. Once she sent me these words: "By the power of the Holy Spirit you may abound and be overflowing (bubbling over) with hope" (Romans 15:13 Amplified).

God is using His Word, spoken by this faithful spiritual mother, to cause hope to bubble up in my soul.

Virginia's Story

"Come, let us sing for joy to the Lord; let us shout aloud . . ." This exhortation from Psalm 95:1 mocked me when I was admitted as a patient to a mental hospital. I did not feel like singing for joy. I did not feel like singing at all. I felt no encouragement, no joy, no peace.

My one-and-a-half-year battle with depression after my son's birth had left me fearful and exhausted. What other people jokingly called "the baby blues" had dragged on until I could barely eat or sleep. Neither could I enjoy my baby. When I held him, I felt intense shyness, guilt, and grief.

My mind grew cloudier and cloudier until I had trouble doing even the simplest tasks. Eventually I wore out. Struggling to get out of bed one morning, I knew it was time to go to a hospital. Things could not continue like this.

At the hospital, I learned that God's encouragement can reach even the most godless places. I shared a room with a woman who was suicidal and met substance abusers, violent ex-prisoners, and people with multiple mental disorders who seemed possessed. I learned, however, that even in such hellishness, God was able not only to encourage me but to use my broken life to encourage others!

Into my life He brought several praying Christians from my church, and He encouraged me through music. As I read my Bible in the hospital, I kept noticing verses urging me to sing, many from the Psalms. I do not have a trained voice, and I had never sung a solo, but in the privacy of my room I began singing softly about Jesus. Gradually I sang a little louder. Then I started singing when I was around the other patients. It was very scary, but the more I stepped out in faith, the more encouraged I became.

My singing soon convinced the nurses and doctors that I was indeed crazy, and when the staff thinks you're crazy, they hesitate to discharge you! The other patients, however, responded very positively to my music. An eighteen-year-old girl who had attempted suicide asked me to sing "Amazing Grace." As she listened, she cried and then asked me to sing it again and again. Afterward she was willing to pray with me. An elderly man often asked me to sing with him, and it was only during those periods of singing that he broke out of his depression. On similar occasions, God used my singing to minister to many others around me.

Then God gave me a roommate who had sung professionally for the San Diego Opera. Although intimidated, I sang for her when she asked, and she exclaimed, "You have a beautiful soprano voice!" Only God could have orchestrated such an encouraging meeting! How amazing it was to see God use my meager talent to encourage others, which then encouraged me.

After a month-long stay, I was discharged from the hospital, and since then God has used my harrowing experience to help me and one of my prayer partners (also a musician) write a song about His healing strength.

My recovery has been slow, but God continues to heal and encourage me through His Word, friends, and music. I am so grateful for what He did!

Encouragement Principle 7

Biblical encouragement builds confidence and results in increased ministry opportunities.

In your own circle of influence are people—children, teens, and adults—who need courage, spirit, and hope. The encouragement you offer could be as simple as a love note in a lunch bag or as complex as a year-long commitment to come alongside a harried young mother. It could be cheering on your child in his first soccer game or telling your church leaders that you appreciate the tough stands they take.

Unless we remember Paul's words in 2 Corinthians 4:7, "But we have this treasure [the gospel] in jars of clay to show that this all-surpassing power is from God and not from us," we will succumb to discouragement due to our own inadequacy when we observe the enormous needs surrounding us. God wants to break apart our jars of clay to display the treasure of the gospel. That process showcases His power and not our weaknesses. This should give us great hope and help us move from "I just don't know how to be an encourager" to "Wow! God really is using me to accomplish His purposes!"

Is there a way to encourage some people without feeling guilty that we have not encouraged everyone? Can we read the weekly prayer list without feeling responsible for every need? Was Deborah's condemnation of the neglectful Israelites a warning that every believer must take personal responsibility for every need? How do we know if God wants us to walk into a situation requiring special skills even though we've had no personal experience from which to glean wisdom? And how do we live the lifestyle of an encourager without being overcome by "compassion fatigue"?

In 2 Corinthians 8:1–5, we find some answers. This passage describes the Macedonians' response to the material needs of the Jerusalem saints—people they probably did not know:

> And now, brothers, we want you to know about the grace that God has given the Macedonian churches. Out of the most severe trial, their overflowing joy and their extreme poverty welled up in rich generosity. For I testify that they gave as much as they were able, and even beyond their ability. Entirely on their own, they urgently pleaded with us for the privilege of sharing in this service to the saints. And they did not do as we expected, but they gave themselves first to the Lord and then to us in keeping with God's will.

If we review the reasons for neglecting encouragement (see chapter 1), we see that the ways to overcome them are in this passage.

1. *Our own lives are full of urgent demands.* The Macedonians gave joyfully and generously although in severe trial and extreme poverty.

2. *We don't know what to say or do, so we decide it is better to say or do nothing than to say or do the wrong thing.* They did not merely give what they were able but sacrificially.

3. *We give up when our initial efforts show no results.* They considered the opportunity to help carry the burden of their spiritual family a privilege and begged to be included.

4. *We are insensitive.* Their giving was an act of worship in that they gave themselves first to the Lord and then to the saints in keeping with God's will. When we give ourselves to God before we try giving ourselves to others, He multiplies our meager offerings and thus we have no reason to worry about how far our encouragement is spreading.

As we become more intimate with Christ, we learn to recognize His voice (John 10:3, 27), and when we respond to His promptings we will find ourselves meeting needs of which we were completely unaware.

Many of us struggle because we do not do what we already know is right. Chuck Swindoll wrote about this in the context of marriage:

> Let me mention one more "cheap substitute" so common among Christian wives in our day. It is learning about what is right rather than doing what is right. It has been my observation that a large percentage of Christian wives know more—much more—than they put into practice. And yet, they are continually interested in attending another class, taking another course, reading another book, going to another seminar . . . learning, discussing, studying, discovering . . . and with what results? Normally, greater guilt. Or, on the other side, an enormous backlog

> of theoretical data that blinds and thickens the conscience rather than spurs it into action. Learning more truth is a poor and cheap substitute for stopping and putting into action the truth already learned.[1]

Perhaps we could make the same observation about ourselves. Some of us attend Bible studies regularly, but do we apply what we are learning? In his exhortation to the Philippians to press on toward the goal of maturity in Christ, Paul said, "Only let us live up to what we have already attained" (Philippians 3:16).

Or, in the words of the well-known sports company Nike: "Just do it!" Just do what God tells you to do. Nothing more. Nothing less.

My friend Sally brought great emotional baggage into her relationship with Christ. Due to some bad choices early in her life, she had little self-esteem. When she came to Christ, she couldn't think of anything she had to offer Him.

The only "special ability" she knew she had was loving and caring for children. So, after being challenged by the teaching of her church to express what Christ had accomplished in her, Sally opened a day-care center. She informed the parents that she was a committed Christian and that her care would expose the children to biblical principles.

God transformed Sally's day care into a mission field. One young mother, Terry, wrote this expression of gratitude:

> One month after our son was born, my husband needed me to come back to work in his business. A church friend told me about Sally, who agreed to care for our little boy. I cried all the way to work the first morning I left him, but I knew he was safe and secure with a Christian mom who knew more about babies than I did. Thankfully, I was able to stay at home when he was seven months old. But, for the next two years Sally was my mothering mentor. She always took time to answer my questions no matter how

1 Charles R. Swindoll, *Strike the Original Match* (Portland, Ore.: Multnomah, 1980), 72.

> silly they may have seemed to her. She never made fun of my ignorance. Instead she pointed me to the One who created our son. God placed Sally in my life at a critical juncture. In this mentoring relationship I grew to the point that the Lord could use me to minister to others.

Linda was a young mother who had no knowledge of the Savior. Not only did Sally love Linda's children, she extended a warm friendship to Linda as well. Soon Sally and her husband began to include Linda and her family in special activities. They also invited them to church. There they saw love in action as they witnessed the special concern Sally's church friends had for one another. This caring attitude drew Linda to God like a magnet, just as Jesus promised (see John 13:34–35). Like a midwife easing a new baby from the mother's body into the world, Sally and her church friends slowly and lovingly eased Linda into God's salvation. Soon Linda's husband and children also gave their lives to Jesus.

Biblical encouragement in the body of Christ is powerful evangelism. When Sally did what she knew *how* to do (care for children), God multiplied her gifts. The women who are rooted in His love because of Sally, are now doing the same for their families and for other young women.

Although Sally still feels inadequate at times, her godly confidence grows every time she takes a deep breath and moves forward to use her gifts to encourage young moms.

Some of you are thinking, *I could never do that*. And you're right. You couldn't. But you're not supposed to. Your ministry will be unique because it will stem from the one-of-a-kind abilities God has given you. God did not create cookie-cutter Christians. Listen to Paul describe the giftedness of the body:

> The body is a unit, though it is made up of many parts; and though all its parts are many, they form one body. So it is with Christ. For we were all baptized by one Spirit into one body—whether Jews or Greeks, slave or free—and we were all given the one Spirit to drink.

> Now the body is not made up of one part but of many. If the foot should say, "Because I am not a hand, I do not belong to the body," it would not for that reason cease to be part of the body. And if the ear should say, "Because I am not an eye, I do not belong to the body," it would not for that reason cease to be part of the body. If the whole body were an eye, where would the sense of hearing be? If the whole body were an ear, where would the sense of smell be? But in fact God has arranged the parts in the body, every one of them, just as he wanted them to be. If they were all one part, where would the body be? As it is, there are many parts, but one body.
>
> The eye cannot say to the hand, "I don't need you!" And the head cannot say to the feet, "I don't need you." On the contrary, those parts of the body that seem to be weaker are indispensable, and the parts that we think are less honorable we treat with special honor. And the parts that are unpresentable are treated with special modesty, while our presentable parts need no special treatment. But God has combined the members of the body and has given greater honor to the parts that lacked it, so that there should be no division in the body, but that its parts should have equal concern for each other. If one part suffers, every part suffers with it; if one part is honored, every part rejoices with it.
>
> Now you are the body of Christ, and each one of you is a part of it. (1 Corinthians 12:12–27)

This passage is one of many that shows believers how we are connected to a body in which each part is responsible for the well-being of all the other parts. None of us is more important than another, and each of us is gifted. If one of us fails to use our God-given gifts or neglects our responsibilities, we deny the truth of Scripture, and we deny the other members the care and nurturing God meant them to receive through us.

Jesus expressed this truth in the parable of the talents (Matthew 25). A man was about to go on a long trip. After carefully considering the abilities of three of his servants, he entrusted them with talents or silver coins "each according to his ability" (v. 15). Two of the servants invested and doubled the treasures. The third servant buried the master's money. When the master returned, he applauded the two faithful servants with the words, "Well done, good and faithful servant! You have been faithful with a few things; I will put you in charge of many things. Come and share your master's happiness!" (Matthew 25:23). He then condemned the faithless servant, saying,

> Take the talent from him and give it to the one who has the ten talents. For everyone who has will be given more, and he will have an abundance. Whoever does not have, even what he has will be taken from him. And throw that worthless servant outside, into the darkness, where there will be weeping and gnashing of teeth. (Matthew 25:28–30)

This passage expresses four life-changing truths:

1. *God gives each of us gifts "according to our abilities," and He expects us to invest them in a way that will build up His kingdom.*
2. *We are stewards of God's gifts, and He will hold us accountable for the way we use them.*
3. *Neither the perceived value of the gift nor the amount of the return is the issue. The issue is our faithfulness in investing rather than consuming or hoarding.*
4. *When we invest His gifts for good, He will offer us expanded opportunities for service.*

This awesome responsibility could terrify us were it not for the promises Jesus gave in John 13–17. Knowing His time was short and "having loved his own who were in the world, he now showed them the full extent of his love" (John 13:1).

The description of Jesus' last days with His disciples leaves no doubt about His great love for them. We see His love in acts of servanthood—He put on an apron and washed their feet. We hear His love in words of assurance—He acknowledged their fear and promised them they would one day understand (John 13:7).

In response to this great love, we are to do four things:

1. *Take the risk of loving others.*

   A new command I give you: Love one another. As I have loved you, so you must love one another. (John 13:34)

2. *Identify ourselves as His own.*

   By this all men will know that you are my disciples, if you love one another. (John 13:35)

3. *Work through doubt and uncertainty until our faith is crystal clear.*

   Jesus replied, "You do not realize now what I am doing, but later you will understand." (John 13:7)

   But the Counselor, the Holy Spirit, whom the Father will send in my name, will teach you all things and will remind you of everything I have said to you. (John 14:26)

4. *Mirror His image; reflect His loving heart to a hurting world.*

   Now that I, your Lord and Teacher, have washed your feet, you also should wash one another's feet. I have set you an example that you should do as I have done for you. I tell you the truth, no servant is greater than his master, nor is a messenger greater than the one who sent him. Now that you know these things, you will be blessed if you do them. (John 13:14–17)

Jesus not only told His disciples to practice love; He promised to give the Holy Spirit as their source of personal encouragement, thus enabling them to love others.

Perhaps you have responded to God's call to encourage with the same confusion and disbelief of the disciples. Jesus never promised their lives would be easy or pain-free. He prepared them for the worst. Just as He did not expect them to satisfy His expectations in their own strength, He does not expect us to be biblical encouragers in our own strength. Jesus' expectations require of us the use of certain spiritual muscles. He does not leave us without equipping us to fulfill our calling.

Covering all these expectations is His promise to send the Counselor, or the *paraclete*: "I will ask the Father, and he will give you another Counselor to be with you forever. . . . I will not leave you as orphans; I will come to you" (John 14:16, 18).

In the last hours of His earthly life, Jesus made a pact with the disciples. His responsibility was to empower them (John 15:26–27, 16:12–15; Acts 1:8); their responsibility was to carry on His work of love.

At Pentecost, Jesus fulfilled His part of the pact. He gave the disciples the gift of the Holy Spirit (Acts 2:1–4), and the frightened men who had left their Messiah and friend to die alone were suddenly filled with courage and power. Truly the Holy Spirit broke the clay pots of their lives and revealed the rich treasures of the gospel.

Is the same power available to us today? Because of certain abuses of the doctrine of the Holy Spirit, we often shy away from acknowledging His role in our lives. Doing so stunts our growth.

The Greek word most often used in Scripture for the Holy Spirit comes from the verb *parakaleo*, which means to "come alongside of." It is often translated "encourage." The Holy Spirit is the encourager who comes alongside, enabling believers to use their gifts, talents, resources, and circumstances to lead the elect to God.

If our calling is to reflect the glory of God and to enjoy Him forever, and the purpose of the Holy Spirit is to point us to Christ (John 16:13), then we must recognize the power of the Holy Spirit in our walk with Christ.

Here is how the Word of God describes this aspect of the role of the Holy Spirit:

> I keep asking that the God of our Lord Jesus Christ, the glorious Father, may give you the Spirit of wisdom and revelation, so that you may know him [God] better. (Ephesians 1:17)

> However, as it is written: "No eye has seen, no ear has heard, no mind has conceived what God has prepared for those who love him"—but God has revealed it to us by his Spirit. The Spirit searches all things, even the deep things of God. . . . We have not received the spirit of the world but the Spirit who is from God, that we may understand what God has freely given us. (1 Corinthians 2:9–12)

Paul exhorted the Philippians to continue to obey what they already knew:

> [Not in your own strength] for it is God Who is all the while effectually at work in you—energizing and creating in you the power and desire—both to will and to work for His good pleasure and satisfaction and delight. (Philippians 2:13 Amplified)

He promised them that God would provide the desire and power for obedience as they were faithful. Peter exclaimed that God provides every guidance we need to satisfy His calling for us:

> His divine power has given us everything we need for life and godliness through our knowledge of him who called us by his own glory and goodness. Through these he has given us his very great and precious promises, so that through them you may participate in the divine nature and escape the corruption in the world caused by evil desires. (2 Peter1:3–4)

That same power is available to everyone who practices biblical encouragement.

How do we overcome our insecurities? By practicing biblical encouragement in the power of the Holy Spirit.

1. *Root yourself in Christ and in His Word.* Discover who you are in Him. Surrender to Christ's calling (John 13–17) and believe that He has equipped you to succeed. In His last words to His disciples, Jesus defined for them their calling—to glorify Him. He did not leave them without the power and ability to fulfill that calling.

Many of us want our lives to grow the fruit of the Spirit, but we are unwilling to abide in Christ, which is the only way it can develop (see John 15:7).

2. *Pray in faith and expect the Holy Spirit to direct you.* Start small, but practice at least one act of encouragement every day. Do what you know is right and live each moment of the day expecting His guidance. Make the same commitment one day at a time.

3. *Define your circle of influence.* In one sense, all of us have a "ready-made" circle of influence—family members, members of the church body, coworkers, neighbors, and all of the people who need the expertise we have gained through similar circumstances. (I meet periodically with other bereaved mothers and we encourage one another.)

We cannot be all things to all people. We must know the people in whom God wants us to invest the most.

Ask God to reveal to you what person needs your ministry of encouragement. If you are a wife and mother, your priority must be to create an encouraging environment in your home. Then you may prayerfully add others.

I am committed to the spiritual-mothering mandate, so I especially encourage my daughter and daughter-in-law and the other members of my young married women's Bible study group. I know I cannot meet the needs of all our church women, so I trust God to raise up other women in our church to focus on the needs of other groups.

Stay focused, but be flexibile so the Holy Spirit can direct you to other opportunities. The focus of our encouragement changes according to our season of life.

4. *Obey quickly*. Jesus promised guidance. Believe Him! Upon hearing of a need, especially of a close friend, make a phone call to say, "I know and I care." Follow up with more love later. If thoughts about a particular friend keep coming to mind, act on them. Pray for her. Send a card telling her you are thinking about her. Call and ask what her needs are. Often God moves us to meet needs that only He could know about. Do not miss these opportunities to see God doing soul work. Each time we obey, God opens other avenues of ministry.

5. *Practice*. Every skill requires practice, even the skill of encouragement. Start small and be willing to serve where you have not served before. Do not be afraid to fail. Remember, Jesus called His disciples to be risk-takers and then gave us the ultimate safety net: the Holy Spirit. Sometimes we will make mistakes, but God will use our obedience to fulfill His purposes. The more we practice being sensitive, the more sensitive we will become. A wise woman will practice in the routines of life, knowing God will honor her obedience in the little things.

Oswald Chambers, one of my favorite devotional writers, said:

> The great hindrance in spiritual life is that we will look for big things to do. "Jesus took a towel . . . and began to wash the disciples' feet."
>
> There are times when there is no illumination and no thrill, but just the daily round, the common task. Routine is God's way of saving us between our times of inspiration. Do not expect God always to give you His thrilling minutes, but learn to live in the domain of drudgery by the power of God.
>
> It is the "adding" that is difficult. We say we do not expect God to carry us to heaven on flowery beds of ease, and yet we act as if we did! The tiniest detail in which I obey has all the omnipotent power of the grace of God behind it. If I do my duty, not for duty's sake, but because I believe God is engineering my circumstances, then at the

very point of my obedience the whole superb grace of God is mine through the Atonement!"[2]

6. *Observe how others encourage*. Start with Jesus. See what He said and did at the tomb of Lazarus. He went to be with His friends even though He could have healed Lazarus from a distance. He wept with them. He gave them hope by pointing them to the Resurrection.

Look for someone in your church who has the reputation of an encourager. Watch her with her children, her husband, and her friends. While maintaining an awareness of your own gifts, allow the Holy Spirit to teach you through her example.

7. *Prepare to encourage*. Jesus anticipated people's needs and moved to meet them before anyone voiced them. He built a fire, made food, and invited His disciples to join Him for breakfast after a night of fishing (John 21:7–9). He is now preparing a place for us in heaven (John 14:2).

Consider the needs of people in your circle of influence and prepare to meet them. For example, if you will be out of town when a friend has surgery, prepare and deliver a care package before you go. Or send it through another friend. If you know the church choir director faces added pressure during the Christmas season, leave a package of his favorite cookies in his office.

Thelma, an older woman in our church, understood how long Sunday mornings were for my four young children. She often left a freshly baked pastry in our car for the children to eat while awaiting their pastor dad.

Get inside the hearts and minds of the people in your circle of influence. Then act accordingly.

8. *Love people the way they need to be loved, not the way you want to love*. Some people glow with satisfaction when publicly praised. Others prefer private encouragement. Some people like hugs. Others do not. If you don't know how to encourage people in their

2 Oswald Chambers, *My Utmost for His Highest* (Grand Rapids: Discovery House, 1989), June 15.

circumstances, read books, study, or ask others in similar circumstances.

My friend Pat lost a child suddenly. When we lost Mark, our mutual friends asked her how they could minister to us. They assumed the mention of Mark's name would upset us. She surprised them with her advice: "Share your 'Mark stories' with them." Pat understood our need better than most, and wise friends tapped into her understanding.

9. *Know your spiritual gift.* Your encouragement ministry will be the most effective if you practice it in the area of your giftedness. There are many fine books about spiritual gifts, so I will not address this subject in detail here. However, a personal study of the "gift passages" will remind you that God gives gifts and talents to each of us for the purpose of building up His body.

10. *Cultivate a servant's heart.* God will expand your circle of ministry when you are willing to "get your hands dirty." Some of your greatest joys will come when you no longer limit your ministry to areas in which you are comfortable.

Anna's Story

The life of Anna (Luke 2) shows us how God used a seemingly insignificant woman in a significant way because she submitted herself to His service.

We don't know what Anna dreamed of doing with her life when she was a young girl; we only know where God placed her. After seven years of marriage, Anna's husband died, but instead of becoming bitter after his death and burying with him her opportunity to glorify God, Anna devoted her life to prayer in the temple, worshiping night and day, fasting and praying. She submitted her life to God, accepting her husband's death as a "talent" entrusted to her by Him, and did what she could to serve Him in the circumstances of His choice.

When Luke wrote about her, she was eighty-four years old.

During her years of prayer and worship, Anna learned the mind and heart of God, so when she saw the baby Jesus in the arms of

His earthly parents, she recognized Him immediately and "gave thanks to God and spoke about the child to all who were looking forward to the redemption of Jerusalem" (Luke 2:38). What enormous encouragement her words were to the family of God, but especially to Mary and Joseph. Luke reports that Mary treasured all these things in her heart.

God rewarded Anna's godly response to difficult circumstances by allowing her to see the Savior and giving her the opportunity to speak words of encouragement to His earthly parents.

Anna probably considered her life unimportant—a simple clay pot—but she served God wholeheartedly, and her life to this day is still yielding treasures of godliness as we learn about faithfulness from her example.

As a child, I thought the parable of the talents described the use and misuse of material possessions. But now I believe the talents are every resource, circumstance, and ability God gives to us.

After one of my encouragement workshops, a tearful woman approached me and said, "I don't know how you can talk about Mark."

"Have you experienced a similar loss?" I asked.

With enormous effort and anguish, she replied, "My own daughter died many years ago, and I never talk about her. I can't."

Later, one of her friends told me that the women of her church never knew about this child until the woman's husband died and was buried beside their dead daughter.

God used this woman's grief and the parable of the talents to again confront me with a choice. Would I, like the evil servant, bury, along with my son's earthly body, every ministry opportunity, or would I believe that God gave me this "talent" as an opportunity to invest it for His glory?

Surely Anna, like me, would not have chosen the death of a loved one as her preferred way of displaying God's grace. Yet God, because of Anna's intimacy with Him, was able to encourage His people through her.

Every one of our circumstances and abilities is a talent entrusted to us by God to use for His glory. And our lives, the clay pots that contain the treasure of the gospel, can be used as containers in which we either bury the gifts God has given or plant them so they will grow and bloom.

Getting Focused

1 Describe the areas of ministry in which you are most comfortable.

2 What fears keep you from broadening your ministry?

Staying Focused

Day One

1 How willing are you to practice encouragement outside the areas in which you are comfortable?

2 Read Matthew 25:14–30. What do the talents symbolize? What are your talents? What steps do you need to take to invest them in the lives of others?

Day Two

1 Spend about thirty minutes reading John 13–17, the passage that contains the words Jesus spoke as He prepared His disciples for His death. Jesus promised that He would not leave them alone and that He would send the Counselor. Ask God to open your heart to the full extent of His love as you meditate on this passage.

Day Three

1 Reread John 13. How did Jesus show the disciples the full extent of His love? What did Jesus expect from His disciples?

Day Four

1 Reread John 13–16. What can the disciples of Jesus expect to experience? How is this relevant to your life? Be specific.

How can God use your circumstances to encourage people in your circle of influence?

Day Five

1 Reread John 13. Of all the things Jesus could do to express His love for His disciples, why did He wash their feet? What was He showing them?

Day Six

1 Reread John 15. What is God's purpose in "pruning" the branches? What branches need to be pruned from your life? Be specific.

Living Focused

Add to your blessing book every circumstance and ability of your life that you consider a "clay pot." Thank God for the way He is going to display His power when you follow Him in obedience.

Remember the "joy box" you gave to a friend? Add an encouragement gem to it.

Chapter Eight

SPIRITUAL MOTHERING

Diane's Story

Imagine an angry and domineering young woman with two confused small children and a husband more concerned with being "Mr. Nice Guy" than with taking his family responsibilities seriously.

This was a portrait of my family.

Into this scene, God sent a godly woman who shared my love for gardening. The two of us often worked together in our yards and, as we did so, she gently worked on my life, nurturing and pruning the branches of my soul. Tilling the ground was hard work, but tilling the hardened soil of my heart was even more difficult. Yet she did not give up on me.

A good gardener knows when to prune, and so she courageously clipped branches of my life when they were sapping the energy needed by developing flower buds.

She was God's heart and hands in my life. Her conversation and attitudes revealed her close relationship with the Master Gardener, and her intimacy with Him gave me a desire to know Him better. From her I learned that husbands and children are ours to enjoy while they are here, but not ours to keep forever. Her gracious submission to God's will taught me how to bow to God's sovereignty in my own circumstances.

She never took my side when I complained about my husband; instead she exhorted me to see him as God's chosen instrument to transform my stubbornness into gentleness. Who but a godly widow could prune self-centeredness from the heart of a young woman by quietly expressing her sadness that her husband was not here? Who but a godly woman could nurture an attitude of gratefulness in my heart by reminding me of my husband's good qualities?

Gardening requires much labor and patience, and the same was true in the garden of my life. Many weeds had grown up, and much growth needed to be pulled out before anything of beauty could be planted. My friend knew how to do both. She cleared away the weeds while keeping in mind the flower of my life that she knew would bloom when planted in the proper conditions.

Her vision for my life gave me hope that my life could be pleasing to God. And because she saw what I could be, knew what I needed, and met the challenge with God's strength, I did eventually blossom into a loving wife and mother.

This godly woman will forever be a symbol of God's love to me.

Encouragement Principle 8

Through biblical encouragement we become spiritual mothers who leave a legacy of hope and courage.

Settling down for our first night of camping at a popular Bible conference ground, my sister, Jane Anne, whispered, "I feel as though I've taken a step back in time. During the church service, I remembered sitting on Mommy's lap in the same building, playing with her necklace. I was Elizabeth's age, about five, and I still remember the necklace. Thinking about that moment makes me feel warm inside."

Peering through the semi-darkness at hanging cobwebs and recalling the countless daddy-long-legs in the showers when we were young, we wondered what memories we would make for our children as we camped with their cousins. Snuggling down in our sleeping bags on that unseasonably cool June night, we heard a whisper coming through the darkness. It was from Elizabeth, Jane's five-year-old. "I have rememories, too, Mommy," she informed us softly. "I have rememories from before tonight and I'm going to have more rememories after this week."

"Rememories." What "rememories" are you making for those around you?

It is frightening to think that, deliberate or not, each of us is leaving a legacy. God has equipped each believer to leave a spiritual heritage of love, courage, and hope, but some women believe they have nothing to offer. When they hear the term *spiritual mothering* they think of a program for which they are ill-prepared rather than a process that leads to godliness.

Susan Hunt, Women in the Church Consultant, Presbyterian Church in America, dispels this thought in the following:

> According to Scripture, the "curriculum" that parents are to teach their children is not found on the pages of a textbook and is not to be taught at 7:00 A.M. The curriculum is a way of life based on biblical truth. You are to "Impress them on your children. Talk about them when you sit at home and when you walk along the road, when you lie down and when you get up" (Deuteronomy 6:7).
>
> In a similar fashion, the spiritual mothering curriculum is to be impressed on younger women as you prepare the fellowship supper together at church, as you make blankets for the home for unwed mothers, as you sort clothes for the homeless shelter, as you talk about how to maintain a devotional life with three preschoolers competing for your attention, as you walk through the factory making deliveries or into the courtroom to defend a client. . . .

> Spiritual mothering has more to do with demonstrating "the shape of godliness" than with teaching lesson plans.[1]

Spiritual mothering takes place when . . .

> a woman possessing faith and spiritual maturity enters into a nurturing relationship with a younger woman in order to encourage and equip her to live for God's glory.[2]

Rather than duplicate studies done by others on spiritual mothering, this book will look at examples of women who demonstrate "the shape of godliness" through biblical encouragement. By observing their lives, we will learn how to nurture our own family of spiritual daughters.

When our congregation sent my husband and me to Hawaii for our twenty-fifth wedding anniversary, we visited Punchbowl Cemetery. Although my journal entry speaks of mother-child relationships, the actions described also symbolize the nurturing relationship between spiritual mothers and daughters:

> Eerie stillness increases the emotion exploding in my soul as this quiet place reminds me of all the mothers whose sons lie buried here. I try to hide sudden tears when I read the tribute Abraham Lincoln gave to Mrs. Bixby, a mother who lost five sons in the Civil War. The words are inscribed under a huge statue of a woman I assume represents all sacrificial mothers. Her oversized hands intrigue me. They seem too big for the statue. . . . Did the craftsman use size to emphasize the ministry of a mother's hands? Consider where nurturing mothers' hands go.
>
> Changing diapers, washing bottoms and faces, cleaning vomit, wiping tears, caressing soft heads, softly placing sleeping bodies in a cradle, swooping up the six month old and swirling her around in a joyful dance, later grabbing

1 Susan Hunt, *Spiritual Mothering* (Franklin, Tenn.: Legacy Communications, 1992), 67.

2 Ibid., 12.

> the arms of the awkward adolescent and dancing around the kitchen, happily squeezing the cheeks of her chubby baby, touching a child's shoulder as she passes, grabbing a preschooler's arm to keep him from running into traffic, deflecting a ball, lovingly preparing favorite foods, setting a lovely table, making Christmas stockings, tying together clover flowers to make a bracelet for her little girl, crocheting a baby blanket or an afghan for a college student, writing letters to children far away, or hands clenched in anger over the hurt a child unjustly experiences, hands firmly clasping a steering wheel while chauffeuring children or tightly grasping her seat as her teen learns how to drive, cradling her teenage son's head as he sobs over a broken heart; hands preparing a safe place for all who enter, big strong hands planting, weeding, cultivating and then picking and canning vegetables and fruit for the winter, not only in her backyard garden but in the garden of her child's heart.
>
> Hands proudly cupping a son's strong jawline on his wedding day or adjusting a cherished daughter's wedding veil, and hands gently combing through a sixteen-year-old son's thick, curly hair as his body rests in his casket, far too soon for her to understand.
>
> Applauding hands, disciplining hands, exhorting hands, loving hands, grieving hands, hands of protection and provision, hands of love, big, rough hands, or small and delicate, hands made strong with self-sacrifice, each finger tightly wound around the life of her child; each finger gently unclenched by the hands of God when it's time to let go.

Although this is a description of a mother nurturing her biological children, God calls women to nurture spiritual children in much the same way.

Judy is an example of a woman who has caught this vision. When I asked her to serve on a spiritual-mothering panel for a conference, she chuckled and said, "I don't know why you want me. I'm just living my life."

I smiled and said, "Your response proves you're just the woman we're looking for. A friend of yours told me of women who would wait in line to applaud the ministry you have had to them over the years."

Judy did not know she was creating a family of spiritual daughters. Although she does not call what she does "spiritual mothering," she is a clear example of the scriptural mandate in Titus 2:3–5, which some call the spiritual-mothering curriculum:

> Likewise, teach the older women to be reverent in the way they live, not to be slanderers or addicted to much wine, but to teach what is good. Then they can train the younger women to love their husbands and children, to be self-controlled and pure, to be busy at home, to be kind, and to be subject to their husbands, so that no one will malign the word of God.

Oswald Chambers described this kind of life with these words:

> I am called to live in perfect relation to God so that my life produces a longing after God in other lives, not admiration for myself.[3]

Judy, according to the testimony of her friend, is committed to God, which produces a longing after God in the women whose lives she touched. Her intimacy with Christ flows over into her encouragement ministry to women.

Spiritual mothering does not just benefit the recipient. Women often discover that their own need to be needed is met through the practice of spiritual mothering. The spiritual benefits are great.

Here's what Jackie has to say on that subject:

> Although many young women are blessed by older women mentoring them, my story is from the older woman's

3 Oswald Chambers, My *Utmost for His Highest* (Grand Rapids: Discovery House, 1989), December 2.

> perspective. The spiritual-mothering mandate in Titus 2:3–5 provides a framework for me to exercise the gifts God has given to me. Without younger women willing to be mentored, I would not have the privilege and joy of teaching them what I have learned from God's Word. Through the love for God's Word poured into my heart by Him, I have had opportunities to disciple younger women in small group Bible studies and individually. My own love for God grows when I see these young women excited about what they've learned from Scripture. It is thrilling to see their lives change and mature because they have applied the truth. I know that the small group Bible study members don't need me. I need them. I'm the one who really benefits. When I am not involved in a structured mentoring relationship or leading a small group, my life is dry. I've learned that when I don't exercise the gifts God has given to me, I become sluggish, lacking in vitality, zeal, and enthusiasm. I am so thankful that God equips and enables me to serve Him by ministering to other women. I am especially grateful for all the women who allow me to encourage them in the study of God's Word. He uses the spiritual mothering framework to nurture my love for Him, His Word, and the joy of sharing with others.

Jackie's story reminds us that God often accomplishes more than one goal with His commands. He uses the obedience of the spiritual mother to meet not only the cravings of the spiritual daughter but also those of the spiritual mother.

During breakfast at a conference where I was speaking, a twice-widowed woman told her personal history of losses and ended with these haunting words:

> I am so lonely. The church is just as neglectful today toward widows as it was when I lost my first husband thirty years ago at the age of twenty-three. Couples we regularly socialized with don't include me anymore and I'm the odd

> man out at church activities. One hostess actually told me she didn't know where I fit in at a church dinner, so I walked out and never went back. Do you know how eerily quiet a house is when you are the only one in it? I dread the loneliness of the dinner table. It's so hard for me to get up in the morning. What purpose do I have? For the first time in my life, no one needs me. My attendance at this conference is a test. How will people treat me? If I don't feel welcome, I'm leaving.

Her tight voice and shiny tears revealed the freshness of her pain, even though her second husband had died several years earlier. The continuing neglect of her church angered me, and I wanted to relieve her anguish. Everything I suggested she do to resolve her longings, she had already done without any good results. This precious woman had a legacy of God's faithfulness to pass on to other women, but her disappointment with the institutional church blinded her to the possibilities.

As she talked, God reminded me that the spiritual mothering mandate is not only for the good of the younger woman. God could satisfy the needs in this woman's life if she had the opportunity to use the treasures of her wisdom to satisfy the longings in another woman's heart.

I suggested to my new friend that God could meet her craving to be needed through a spiritual-mothering ministry. Since her church leaders were not responding to her cries for help, perhaps she should change her focus. Instead of concentrating on the neglect of the institutional church, why not consider how she could minister as a part of the body? When she stared at me in what I perceived as disagreement and surprise, I thought perhaps I had misread God's leading. However, later that week she joyfully rushed up to me, her countenance glowing, and rattled off this story:

> I spent several hours listening to another woman share her sad life history. I was able to minister to her by sharing from

> my own story. I think I really helped. I am so excited that God used me this way. He really does want to use me.

I know this woman has a long journey into healing, but I am convinced that helping others is the quickest and surest way to get there. Will it be easy? No. Initially, obedience is hard, but in the long run, disobedience is harder. And continuing to allow bitterness to grow will be excruciating.

Here's what Lisa says about it:

> I was an adult when God saved me. My first two years as a Christian were a wild roller coaster ride. My sister, also a new Christian, saw my discouragement and knew what I needed to get grounded. She was involved in a Paul-Timothy ministry in which the "Paul" is an older woman who disciples the "Timothy," a younger woman. They suggested that I participate in a one-on-one relationship. Frustrated by my own failures, I agreed. I had attended church sporadically, but I was very shy and felt I wasn't good enough to be there because I was in a class below everyone else. I refused to get involved in any church activities because I feared rejection. But my "Paul" became my best friend. She attended everything offered for women in the church just to get me to go. Our regular meeting times taught me the disciplines of Bible study, prayer, and how to share my testimony. Putting my life under the microscope of Scripture, she continues to help me sort the good from the bad in my life. Through this friendship, God overcame my feelings of intimidation to such a degree that I now sign up for Bible studies, retreats, or other events even if she can't go. It doesn't matter if I don't know anyone because she taught me how to make new friends. I no longer worry that people will think I'm "low class." I've even helped organize special women's events. My friend pointed me to Christ and taught me that He is in me and that I am a child of the King.

A one-on-one discipling relationship is not the only way to fulfill the spiritual-mothering mandate. As we think about the legacy we are leaving, Karen's story reminds us to focus not only on the big events of life, but also on the little things:

> Through the visitation ministry of our church, I came to know God, but I had no idea how to be a godly woman until God gave me the friendship of a spiritual woman. She's not that much older than I am, but I call her my spiritual mother. Although we never had what some people call a "one-on-one" relationship, she taught me all of Titus 2:3–5 simply by the way she lived her life. She frequently invited me to her home and let me learn just by observing her. She invited me to my first small group Bible study and made sure I connected with other women, kept me accountable to study God's Word, prayed with me on the phone, and called three times a week for several months to pray with me about a specific issue.
>
> She encouraged me to get involved in ministry and got me to sign up for nursery duty even through I was scared and hesitant. She consistently exhorted me to deal with facts (not just emotions) and encouraged me to take a hard look at my fears. She taught me to be as bold as a lion in Christ. If I call her in a moment of emotional turmoil, I know she will bring me back to scriptural encouragement.
>
> But Barbie is more than just talk. She lovingly cares for my children when I have physical needs or when I need an overnight break with my husband. She not only babysits when I need to finish a project, but sends me home with a meal as well. She taught me how to handle a newborn, make toddlers take naps, and administer loving discipline. She also taught me how to serve a growing family, host a large group, manage a home, and add structure to my family. Her relationship to her husband teaches me how to love mine. Observing her has taught me poise.

> The impact of this woman's life overwhelms me. I knew nothing about Christianity until God sent her into my life. It's thrilling for me to be able to offer to other women what Barbie offered me. I hope one day to have a legacy of spiritual daughters.

In 2 Corinthians 6:3–4, Paul tells us that we are to

> put no stumbling block in anyone's path, so that our ministry will not be discredited. Rather, as servants of God we commend ourselves in every way; in great endurance; in troubles, hardships and distresses.

Paul lived out his faith, not just in the spotlight or when a big crisis hit, but in the steady, persevering work in the unseen, the mundane things of life, when disruptions were the norm and when hardships and distresses were routine. He did not view pressure and difficulties as reasons to drop out of ministry. Clearly he believed others benefited from seeing him live a purposeful and transparent life. Paul never attempted to disguise his battle with his own sin nature. We are privileged to see the glory of God produced in him *through* hardships, troubles, and distresses, not in the absence of them.

When Barbie came alongside Karen, inviting her to observe her in action, her confidence was not in her ability to be perfect; it was in her identity in Christ. She knew that witnessing the up-and-down realities of family relationships would equip Karen for marriage and motherhood better than a false image of a perfect Christian family. Likewise, when a woman answers the call of spiritual motherhood, she does not need to hide her imperfections or failures. We learn by observing mistakes as well as successes.

The legacy of a spiritual mother is in having spiritual daughters who pass on to others what they have received. Each person is like the next ripple in an ever-widening circle.

When an older woman took special care of me after minor surgery, I asked her how I could thank her. I'll never forget her reply. "Years ago I could not be with my sister when she needed me, and an older Christian woman helped her," she began. "When I asked how I could repay her kindness, she told me to do for someone else what she had done for my sister. Since your mother can't be here, I come in the name of Christ and because I love you. Thank me by doing for someone else what I have done for you."

The greatest tribute we can pay to a spiritual mother is to reflect her love of Christ to others. My friend Denise does just that. When Denise was a young single adult, God impressed upon her the need to have an older mentor. For several years she arranged her schedule to take advantage of a women's Bible study offered by her church and there absorbed many aspects of godliness. Although she has never married and has no children of her own, she nurtures many young girls who come to her for horseback riding lessons. As she works side by side with the girls, they see the difference Christ makes in a woman whose heart is committed to Him. Frequently I see Denise at church and youth events with several young girls in tow. She is exposing them to the community of Christ. Denise, the spiritual daughter of many women, is now building her own legacy of spiritual daughters. The circle of influence is ever widening.

Another friend, Susan, longs for a spiritual mother but is unable to find one. Here is her story:

> I am one of those first-generation Christians. I am in desperate need of a spiritual mother and have been praying for God to send me one. I do not know what a close relationship with an older woman, let alone a Christian woman, would be like. I must admit, one sin I continually confess to God is jealousy and coveting what I see in other Christian homes for my own family.

If you share such a need and there is no one to be your mentor, turn to books by Christian women; they can serve as a spiritual mother through their writings. Although I have never met Elisabeth Elliot or Amy Carmichael, I consider them spiritual mothers. Amy Carmichael influenced my response to cancer and Elisabeth

Elliot influenced my response to Mark's death. Other writers and speakers continue to shape my thinking in significant ways.

Serving in the church and on committees also exposes me to godly women. Although it is different from a mentoring relationship, we are discipling one another by the way we serve and respond to our work.

Don't close your heart to the treasures of encouragement God has for you. Refuse the urge to define for Him how He must meet the longings of your heart. If you are a child of the King, you have treasures to offer and riches to discover.

My challenge to you is this: instead of focusing on your needs, ask God to direct you to the person you can influence. You are probably thinking, "I don't know anyone who needs me." I suggest you volunteer for the church nursery and prayerfully ask God to bring into your life a young woman who needs to be loved. You need not commit to a weekly one-on-one Bible study; you only need to commit to a loving relationship that reveals who you are in Christ. Perhaps your familiar, smiling face on Sunday mornings will allow her to listen more attentively during the service. What about telling her how precious her children are and what a good job she is doing raising them. Perhaps you could invite her to a special event. If she can't go because she needs a baby-sitter, offer to take care of her children while she goes with another friend—your treat. Mentoring opportunities abound for Sunday school teachers, children, and youth workers.

Do these suggestions make you uncomfortable? Remember the Israelites who refused to take risks.

Are you spinning a self-protective cocoon around yourself or are you asking God for opportunities to connect with those who need a godly example?

Is there a young woman who needs a grandmother in her life—maybe your own granddaughter?

At a women's conference, Susan Hunt told the story of a grandmother who set out to cultivate a spiritual mothering relationship with her grandchildren. When one of them was chosen as Outstanding Young Woman of the Year, a television reporter interviewed her. After listing all of her exemplary activities and commenting on her commitment to purity, the reporter asked, "How do you resist the temptation to use drugs, drink, or get involved in sexual immorality?" The lovely young cheerleader smiled impishly and replied, "Whenever I'm tempted to do something wrong, I see my grandmother's face, and I just can't do it!"

What a legacy this grandmother is leaving! How I pray that one day my own grandchildren will respond similarly. This grandmother took seriously her role as a spiritual mother.

We may slip into another woman's life for a short time. Our ministry may be temporary or long distance. Just as encouragement is not an option for the child of God, neither is spiritual mothering. If the Holy Spirit is convicting you about your need to encourage others, spiritual mothering is a satisfying way to respond to that conviction.

In every woman's life there should be a two-fold process of mentoring, that is, older women who are mentoring her as well as younger women she is mentoring. If you are committed to nurturing younger women, surround yourself with women who mentor you. Again, that mentoring may take place in a one-on-one relationship, through books and speakers, or in a group. But ask God to give you at least one other mature woman who will sharpen you "as iron sharpens iron" (Proverbs 27:17).

Spiritual mothering energizes, but also depletes. As we empty ourselves to nurture others, God fills us through the ministry of the body.

My friend Linda, who lost a child through death, worried that she was neglecting the needs of others as she learned to walk the pathway of grief. She confessed to a friend, "I just don't have the energy to meet anyone else's needs right now. It's all I can do to get out of bed in the morning. But I feel so guilty."

Wisely, her friend made this analogy:

> Whenever you travel on an airplane, the flight attendant demonstrates the use of the oxygen mask and always tells

> the passengers to put their own mask on before helping a child or elderly person. Linda, you must put on your own oxygen mask before you can help others.

Linda experienced great freedom when she gave herself permission to take time to heal, realizing that doing so would not cheat others of her ministry but would equip her to better assist others in the future. That's good advice for all spiritual mothers.

Sometimes in women's ministries there is conflict between older and younger women. The younger women see established ministries as "sacred cows" that should be lined up and shot. The older women see only immaturity and disrespect in the younger group.

Both groups need to work to overcome this sad state of affairs.

Younger women, understand that the "sacred cows" are sacred for a reason. Perhaps the older women met Christ through their favored ministry, learned how to be a mom, or survived the loss of their spouses. Although their ministry may not be the "hot spot" in the church right now, it was at one time and is precious to them. Is it really necessary to bury it? Consider the Scriptures that proclaim the wisdom of age. Study the Proverbs that challenge young people to listen to their mothers and think of it in terms of listening to spiritual mothers. Ask God to give you a special love and respect for older women.

I often hear younger women complain that the older women don't want to mentor them, but older women have told me they sense closed hearts, and this causes them to think they have nothing worthwhile to offer.

Young women who disrespect the wisdom of older women are cheating themselves of the treasures these women have collected throughout their years. They may also be guilty of pride and narrow-mindedness.

Older women, I know change is hard. The older I get the more stuck in my routines I become. However, I also know that challenges to the way I think and do things are opportunities for me to stretch and expand my offerings to God. If we stay focused on our calling to glorify God, we will not be threatened by new ideas and new methods. We will remember that God is wonderfully creative and that women and their ideas are like the many hues of a rainbow.

When we insist on using all our energy and resources to prop up sacred cows that have outlived their usefulness, aren't we just as prideful and selfish as the ones who want to shoot them?

Wonderful avenues of ministry can be opened by older women who are willing to take the challenge of meeting the needs of younger women. In fact, a heart for ministering to younger women will challenge and deepen your relationship to Christ.

A woman of faith and spiritual maturity is one whose primary goal is to glorify God. If we truly believe this, these conflicts are resolvable.

Spiritual mothering is not necessarily determined by age. When my husband first entered the ministry, I led a women's Bible study. How grateful I am for the elderly women who faithfully attended. I learned so much about the faithfulness of God from their life journeys. I doubt they learned much from me, but they acted as though I was teaching them. I am confident that they put aside many of their own needs to let me cut my teaching teeth on them. They were old enough to be my great grandmothers, but assured me that learning was a two-way process.

I now lead a young married women's Bible study. All of the participants are my daughter's age. Although I call them my spiritual daughters, they are often spiritual mothers to me. I know God is doing soul work in their lives, and I want them to share with me the treasures He is giving to them. Their generation is much more open than mine, and through their discussions I often learn more than I really want to know! But they are teaching me in ways that only they could.

If all of us, older and younger alike, remember that all ministry is God's, not ours, we will have an open hand ready to accept old and new ideas.

Many spiritual mothers continue to teach me how to live. God has also given me two who taught me how to die.

Doctors diagnosed Barbara with a vicious, fast-growing breast cancer shortly after I completed chemotherapy for the same disease. We became fast friends during her months of aggressive treatments, but soon Barbara and I both knew that she had no hope of recovery. As my husband and I prepared to visit her in the hours before her death, I said to him, "I'm scared. I don't know what to say. I love Barbara and I don't want to see her like this."

Instead of staying with me, my husband quietly left us alone. As I sat next to Barbara's bed, she must have sensed my discomfort. She gently took my hand, smiled, and with great peace said, "Sharon, I don't want to go, but I'm ready."

Because Barbara's life had produced in me a longing after God, I knew her words were true. On holy ground we wept and prayed, knowing our next meeting would be in heaven.

At Barbara's memorial service, many of her spiritual daughters expressed how her life had "demonstrated the shape of godliness."

Her response to death encouraged me to trust our Father more deeply.

My aunt Connie, when dying of cancer and in great discomfort, spoke to me of the encouragement God was giving to her.

"When are the trees the most beautiful?" she asked us.

"In the autumn," we answered, "when the leaves are changing color."

"Yes," she replied, "just before the leaves die, they are the loveliest. Just before I die, I want to be the loveliest I have ever been for my Savior. Don't cry for me. I'm the one who is going home. By dying, I live. Though this disease is making me outwardly ugly, I want those who love and know me to remember that I was lovelier in death than in life, just like those autumn leaves before they die. And remember," she added mischievously, "those leaves come back in the spring!"

As she talked, I realized that she was not in a dark, frightening room waiting for God to turn on the lights. Rather, she was following the light of His presence as He led her step by step to the doorway of heaven.

My aunt fulfilled her desires. Consistent, devoted service to Jesus Christ was her signature in life. What a great legacy she left as she died to self and submitted to the disruptions in her journey. In death she left a heritage of hope when she smiled through her pain and reminded us that, just like the falling leaves, she would live again.

I cherish the treasures of encouragement these two women gave from their spiritual inheritance, and every time I invest in a spiritual daughter, their legacy continues.

What "rememories" are you making? What is your legacy? May I suggest that each morning you pray, "Lord, use me to cultivate a compassionate community and produce a longing after You in those around me." Then watch Him work!

Getting Focused

1. Define "spiritual mothering."
2. List women who have influenced you. What did they do to make a difference in your life?
3. Whom do you spiritually mother?

Living Focused

Day One

1. Review your Blessing Book. Spend time in prayer praising God for each treasure listed.
2. Read Titus 2:1–5. List each element in the spiritual-mothering curriculum. Start a page in your Blessing Book for women who demonstrate the shape of godliness to you. State at least one way they impact your life. One by one, tell each one how she has influenced you.

Day Two

1. What is your reaction when you hear the term *spiritual mothering*? Do you consider it an obligation or a privilege?

Ask God to forgive any resentment you have and to give you a desire to become a spiritual mother.

2 Read 2 Corinthians 6:3–4. Are you reluctant to allow another woman into your life because of your own hardships and stresses? Sometimes the best gift we can give is to let another observe us as we struggle through the hard times. What was Paul's motive in living out his faith? What is yours?

Day Three

1 Read Hebrews 10:19–25. List the steps leading to encouragement. Are you neglecting any of them? Be specific. How will you change?

Day Four

1 Start your quiet time praising God for the richness of your inheritance as a child of the King.

2 Read 2 Corinthians 9:6–15. Are you sowing encouragement seeds sparingly? If so, what fruit will they bear? Read verse 8. If God is convicting you to change, what does He promise He will do if you repent?

Day Five

1 Start your quiet time by asking God to keep you focused on Him today. Read 2 Corinthians 9:6–15. What is keeping you from becoming a spiritual mother? If God is calling you to this ministry, what does this passage promise?

2 Make a list of all obstacles to encouragement and ask God how He wants you to overcome them.

Day Six

1 Ask God to open your heart and mind to a specific message from His Word and to direct you to encourage a specific woman.

2 Read 2 Corinthians 9:6–15, paying special attention to

verses 12 and 13. Who will receive the praise for encouragement directed by the Holy Spirit?

3 Ephesians 5:15–16 teaches us to "be very careful, then, how you live—not as unwise but as wise, making the most of every opportunity because the days are evil." How will you make the most of every contact with other women to glorify God?

Living Focused

Purposefully encourage a young woman this week. Send a card, prepare a meal, or offer to baby-sit. If you are a young woman in need of a spiritual mother, make your needs known to an older woman in your church. Ask her to pray about mentoring you. If you simply want an older woman as a friend, invite her to lunch and ask her advice on an issue in your life. Admitting that you need her will encourage her walk with Christ.

Chapter Nine

TREASURES OF THE SOUL

Evelyne's Story

Although I was heartbroken over my daughter's marital problems, it was overwhelming concern for her spiritual welfare that pushed me to my knees. Her husband was involved in a cult religion that I called "God-Man-Satan." Terrible fear for my daughter's spiritual safety engulfed my soul, and I petitioned the Lord to keep her safe. Often during the day I brought this terror to the Lord. When I couldn't sleep or when I'd awaken for no plausible reason—the "call" for prayer was so urgent I could do nothing else.

Finally, I went to see Michal. I do not believe in interfering or in giving unsolicited advice, but I knew the time was right. She knew it too and was waiting for me. I told her the exact words of my prayer for her: "Lord, only You can protect our daughter. It is beyond my help. Please, dear Lord, please, please build a fence around her—a real fence, a barrier—which Satan cannot get through."

Michal was silent for a few minutes, looking at me very strangely—tears making her eyes bright. "Mother," she said, "was that the very wording of your prayer? The very word—'a fence'?"

"Yes," I replied. Silence again.

Then finally, she told her story. "Mother, that explains it! Something baffled Georgie (a self-appointed high priestess with psychic powers). Something stymied her when she prayed for me. These are Georgie's exact words. 'I can't reach her. There is something surrounding her that is so thick and high that I cannot see over it, under it, or through it. I see a fence around her. I can't get through.'"

I felt like falling on my face in awe of God. How great He is—and how gracious of Him to use this means to keep my daughter safe in Him. How much He must care to let me know He heard my prayer. In that very dark hour of spiritual trial, He encouraged me. It was as if I heard Him say, "My little child, I could have protected her without a fence, but I did it this way so you'd be sure that I heard your every word."

Imagination? Oh no, assurance that He cares and hears even me![1]

Heidi's Story

For as long as I can remember, I have longed to have a family with lots of children. In fact, I expected to come home from my honeymoon pregnant! But God had other plans, which I began learning about when a fertility specialist informed me that without medication I would never conceive. Friends and family began praying for God to work through the drugs to give Greg and me a baby. My sister-in-law, Melanie, entered our struggles in a special way through prayer. She was pregnant herself, but whenever people asked how they could pray for her, she would respond, "Just pray for Heidi." She put aside her own joy to enter my pain, and she downplayed her own pregnancy to find out more about my hopes, dreams, and fears.

It was appropriate, therefore, that Melanie was the first person Greg and I told when we found out that we too were going to have a baby. Melanie, then nine months pregnant, grabbed me around the neck and jumped and squealed with joy. God had answered her prayers with a resounding yes! Her niece or nephew was on the way!

Two days later Chuck and Melanie stopped by to continue

1 From the journals of Evelyne Hay Houston. Used with permission.

rejoicing with us. Unfortunately, we had just learned that I was going to miscarry. Melanie sat on my bed and tried not to cry. One week later when I lost my baby, Melanie went through the emotional pain with me. I looked at her and did not feel alone.

Melanie matched her prayer support with practical help. She arranged for friends to deliver meals for a week and sent me a card the day after I lost the baby. Her mother is in heaven with my brother Mark and my baby. Her note said,

> "I am praying to God and asking Him to tell Mommy to please take care of your baby until you get to heaven. She won't be here to help me take care of my baby, but I know she'll do a wonderful job loving your baby . . . temporarily for you."

A friend of my mother's sent me a card with this note:

> "At the loss of a child find comfort in the sovereignty of God. There is no lost potential, no purpose unaccomplished, there is only the glorious plan of God perfectly fulfilled in a precious little life. With prayers that God will comfort your sorrow as we await the day when all things will be clearly understood."

I know God led this spiritual mother, whom I have never met, to write such words. Her message acknowledged my baby's life, however short, gave me a moment to cry, and pointed me toward the sovereign love of God.

Although gravely disappointed by our loss, I felt as if the prayers of the body of Christ were supporting me and holding together the pieces of my broken heart.

The prayer support of my church family also empowered me to be present at the birth of Melanie and Chuck's baby thirteen days after Greg and I lost ours. Many people ask how I could handle such an emotional moment without focusing on my own loss. Because of Melanie's determination to pray me through my valley, I never considered missing her mountaintop experience—the birth of little Mark Nathan Betters, my brother's namesake.

Encouragement Principle 9

Consistent, fervent prayer is the greatest treasure of encouragement we have to offer.

Women committed to the ministry of biblical encouragement learn that they have little to offer if they try to minister without a foundation of prayer. Through prayer we miraculously enter the struggles of others. God moves through our prayers to strengthen the body and to direct our encouragement. Instead of covering ourselves in a cocoon of self-protection, we connect with one another with open hands and outstretched arms. He also reveals His love for us when He moves the body to pray at specific times for specific needs known only to Him. What could be more encouraging than to know that the God of the universe cares about the details of my life?

The ministry of prayer is a mystery. Scripture commands it, the experiences of Christians throughout the ages confirm its force, and even unbelievers espouse its power. Pharaoh repeatedly asked Moses to pray for an end to the plagues. I wonder if one activity of heaven is comparing all our earthly prayer urges with the needs of the people prayed for. If so, I believe we will experience outstanding joy when we learn how God used our prayers to meet specific needs in others—needs only He knew.

The purpose of this chapter is not to explain the mystery or theology of prayer. Many fine volumes already have been written for our instruction. Rather, this chapter is to create in women a hunger to experience the power of prayer and a desire to practice it regularly. We give treasures of the soul when we enter the life of another through Spirit-led prayer.

The need to pray for a young couple overwhelmed me on the first anniversary of the birth of their stillborn child. They were now expecting twins, and my intense urge to pray made me wonder if something was wrong. I whispered, "Lord, whatever their needs are, if they are grieving or if there is something wrong with their babies, please make them aware of Your presence." Arriving home, I called, ready to go to their house if necessary. Instead, I experienced joy when I heard this story.

Because of the history of Down syndrome in their family, the expectant mother had to undergo a test to check the twins' heartbeats. If the heartbeats were strong, they probably did not have Down syndrome. The test had been delayed once and if it was not performed that day, they would have to wait another month. Unfortunately, the doctor could not perform the test because of the babies' positions in the womb. After the doctor left the hospital room, the young husband said, "Honey, I think we should pray that the babies will move so the test can be done." When the doctor returned, he exclaimed, "The babies are in the right position! They moved!" He completed the test and informed the parents that their babies' heartbeats were strong. I realized that at the moment God urged this couple to pray for their babies, He also burdened me to pray. On the anniversary of a day of grief, God gave them a reason for joy.

Although physically separated, God connected us through prayer. Allowing me to participate in such a special moment was God's encouragement treasure to me.

Two months later, two healthy baby boys entered the world.

The Hard Work of Prayer

Paul exhorts us with these words:

> Finally, be strong in the Lord and in his mighty power. Put on the full armor of God so that you can take your stand against the devil's schemes. For our struggle is not against flesh and blood, but against the rulers, against the authorities, against the powers of this dark world and against the spiritual forces of evil in the heavenly realms. Therefore

> put on the full armor of God, so that when the day of evil comes, you may be able to stand your ground, and after you have done everything, to stand. Stand firm then, with the belt of truth buckled around your waist, with the breastplate of righteousness in place, and with your feet fitted with the readiness that comes from the gospel of peace. In addition to all this, take up the shield of faith, with which you can extinguish all the flaming arrows of the evil one. Take the helmet of salvation and the sword of the Spirit, which is the word of God. And pray in the Spirit on all occasions with all kinds of prayers and requests. With this in mind, be alert and always keep on praying for all the saints.
>
> Pray also for me, that whenever I open my mouth, words may be given me so that I will fearlessly make known the mystery of the gospel, for which I am an ambassador in chains. Pray that I may declare it fearlessly, as I should. (Ephesians 6:10–20)

Paul's request for prayer was not a religious cliché. In another passage he implied that we enter one another's struggles through prayer: "I urge you, brothers, by our Lord Jesus Christ and by the love of the Spirit, to join me in my struggle by praying to God for me" (Romans 15:30). Paul yearned to represent Christ courageously, and his request for prayer to this end teaches that we participate in one anothers' lives through the practice of prayer.

The word Paul uses for struggle is *sunagonizomai*, which means "to struggle in company of; i.e., to be a partner (assistant), strive together with."[2] Its root word, *agonizomai*, means "to endeavor to accomplish something: fight, labor fervently, strive," for example, to compete for a prize or to contend with an adversary.[3]

Apparently Paul considered intercessory prayer an opportunity to battle the forces that threaten the honor of Christ. His choice

2 *The New Strong's Exhaustive Concordance of the Bible* (Nashville: Nelson, 1990), 68.

3 Ibid., 8.

of words made clear that any who accepted his invitation to pray were agreeing to hard work. See the word *agonize* in this root word. When you say, "I'll pray for you," are you agreeing to agonize for that person's needs? Are you saying you are willing to become a partner in his or her circumstances? Perhaps the reason we don't pray as we should is because real prayer takes us to the front lines of the spiritual war zone.

Like Reuben's tribe of old, we prefer "whistling for the flocks" (Judges 5:16) rather than engaging a deadly enemy.

The Mysteries of Prayer

Prayer mysteriously connects us to one another emotionally and makes us participants in the soul work God is doing. It gives us a means to express our deep love for one another. Paul often reminded the early church that although he was not physically present, he was supernaturally connected to them through prayer:

> For this reason, since the day we heard about you, we have not stopped praying for you and asking God to fill you with the knowledge of his will through all spiritual wisdom and understanding. And we pray this in order that you may live a life worthy of the Lord and may please him in every way: bearing fruit in every good work, growing in the knowledge of God, being strengthened with all power according to his glorious might so that you may have great endurance and patience, and joyfully giving thanks to the Father, who has qualified you to share in the inheritance of the saints in the kingdom of light. (Colossians 1:9–12)

> I thank my God every time I remember you. In all my prayers for all of you, I always pray with joy because of your partnership in the gospel from the first day until now, being confident of this, that he who began a good work in you will carry it on to completion until the day of Christ Jesus. (Philippians 1:3–6)

Four months after Mark's death, I agreed to give a short devotional at a women's conference about the miracle of the ministry of encouragement. After I spoke, Susan Hunt asked the four hundred women present to pray for continued healing in our lives. When she asked for specific prayer for Chuck, I knew God was using the prayers of these women to meet needs only He could have known. By phone later that evening, Chuck asked me what I was doing from 9:15 to 9:30 that night, and I told him about the prayer time. When I arrived home, he shared this story:

> All alone in our home for the first time since Mark's death, I felt overwhelming anguish and longing for our son. I tried to distract myself by reading, studying, and watching basketball. Nothing worked. I begged God to comfort me, but instead of God's nearness, I felt an ominous murky presence in our home. Finally, I gave up trying to stop the pain and turned out all the lights, matching the black night in my soul with physical darkness. Anguish mounted as the demons of doubt and despair attacked. It was 9:15. Then at 9:30, the ominous darkness was gone. The strangling grief melted. Although I still yearned for Mark, the longing was bearable.

God enlisted four hundred women to enter my husband's struggle and supernaturally chase away the demons of doubt and loneliness. We later learned that God moved a group of young married couples to pray for him at that exact time as well. Was the pain gone, the struggle over? No. But a body of praying believers had helped to carry the burden.

Peace Through the Storm

When Kathy was eight years old, she told her sexually abusive father, "I don't want to live with you anymore. I want to be with Mom." She didn't see him again until twenty-eight years later when God opened the doors for a reunion. Kathy knew that only her heavenly Father could give her the right words to express her feelings to the earthly father who had violated and betrayed her.

I met Christ as a young adult and slowly learned how to forgive my father. I was not bitter or angry, but I was very sad. I knew that our relationship would never heal if I did not lovingly confront him with how his behavior affected me. My memories of that time were so clear that I did not know how I would face him. I called my best friends and asked for prayer.

I tried to play out our first meeting ahead of time. How could I convey Christ's redemption? Could I trust my body to behave? Would ugly memories rise up and overwhelm me? Would his touch stir up old revulsion? I needed wisdom and strength, so I expanded the circle of personal prayer warriors by calling a network of praying friends around the country.

During my first meeting with my father I labored to forgive him. I told him about Christ's work in my life. Then I explained that even though the damage he had done had disrupted my life, God had "restored the years that the locusts had eaten" (Joel 2:25 NKJV). A supernatural gentleness poured out of me that was not from me, not from the little girl who struggled so long with rejection. Instead, the Holy Spirit manifested this truth in my life: "Perfect love casts out fear." In those moments I had no fear, only love for my dad.

That night I lay awake wondering how I had managed to endure the reunion with such grace. Of course! God had worked through faithful prayer warriors!

The next day my dad said, "You did your part yesterday, now I must do mine. I can't tell you how ashamed and sorry I am for what I did. When I thought of it, I wanted to commit suicide. The worst thing is, because of that, I blanked you out of my mind."

We grieved together over his loss of my childhood. And then, instead of bitterness and rage, I felt sorrow for him. The tenderness of God's grace poured out of me and enveloped us both. Again, this grace wasn't from me. It was from Christ, the Wounded Healer, God Incarnate, who was moving us toward restoration.

Spiritual Cheerleading

My husband's softball team was in a critical play-off game. Two outs, and the count on the batter was three balls and two strikes. Boom! The ball zoomed over the heads of the outfielders. A typical ballplayer would easily have rounded all the bases. Unfortunately the hitter was a big man with knee problems. Everyone screamed as he chugged around the bases, huffing and puffing with each step. As he rounded third, I saw Chuck run backwards alongside him down the baseline, yelling, "Come on, Doug, you can do it! Come on, run!" Chuck desperately wanted to grab Doug and drag him to homeplate! But if he did, his team would lose. Chuck's screams made Doug reach deep down inside for that extra strength and we won!

Paul acted as a spiritual cheerleader when he prayed, "With this in mind, we constantly pray for you, that our God may count you worthy of his calling, and that by his power he may fulfill every good purpose of yours and every act prompted by your faith" (2 Thessalonians 1:11). He encouraged their growth with every word.

Chuck and I want to be spiritual cheerleaders for our grandchildren. We have started an album for each of them, and at each one's birth we write a letter expressing our great joy and our anticipation of their growth in Christ. We close the letter with a prayer like this one:

> Dear Father,
>
> We do not stop giving thanks for the birth of our little Mark. We ask you to always give him the Spirit of wisdom and revelation so that he will know You better. We pray also that the eyes of his heart will be enlightened in order that he may know the hope to which You have called him, the riches of Your glorious inheritance in the saints, and Your incomparably great power for him if he believes.

> We kneel before You, Father, and pray that You will strengthen Mark with power through Your Spirit in his inner being so that Christ will dwell in his heart through faith. We pray that You will root and establish him in Your love and show him how wide and long and high and deep is the love of Christ. We want him to know that this love of Yours surpasses knowledge.
>
> Dear Lord, we pray this in order that Mark will live a life worthy of You and will please You in every way. We want him to bear fruit in every good work and grow in knowledge of You. (Ephesians 1:15–19; 3:14–19; Colossians 1:10)

Each year on their birthdays, we add another page to their albums. We want to cheer on their spiritual growth even though we cannot be with them at every step.

Are there children or others in your church who need a spiritual cheerleader? Even when we don't know how to pray, we can pray using words of Scripture and know that we are praying in God's will, cheering on a child of God.

The Direction of Prayer

Through prayer we not only enter one another's spiritual struggles, we also find out how to encourage others in practical ways. When we don't know what to do for another person, God will direct our encouragement through biblical prayer. James 1:5 tells us, "If any of you lacks wisdom, he should ask God, who gives generously to all without finding fault, and it will be given him."

Before Jesus left His disciples, He promised they would not be alone; He would send the Counselor who would guide them into all truth. Jesus' promise to His disciples is repeated in 1 Corinthians 2:12–13:

> We have not received the spirit of the world but the Spirit who is from God, that we may understand what God has freely given us. This is what we speak, not in words taught

> us by human wisdom but in words taught by the Spirit, expressing spiritual truths in spiritual words.

Through Scripture and prayer, the Holy Spirit gives us God's view of another person's need.

Keeping a prayer journal helps me know how and whom to encourage. I write letters to God, asking Him who needs a note, a call, a hug, or some other action from me. I ask Him to bring specific names to mind, and He does give wisdom when I ask. This journal is a record of His intimate participation in my life. When I leave for heaven, my children will know exactly how I prayed for each of them. And they will know how much God and I loved them.

Prayer Connections

To experience a compassionate community requires communication and connection. Communication with God connects us to one another.

My husband and I experienced a new wave of anguish and yearning for Mark on August 4–5, 1994. We felt abandoned by God in a high tide of grief. The mysterious beauty of the Grand Teton Mountains reminded us of our insignificance, and we abruptly ended our sabbatical. Several days after arriving home we received this note from our friend Sandy:

> I am on holiday with my family. On August 4 and 5 God compelled me to constantly pray for you. I don't know where you are or what is happening in your life, but I pray you are feeling His presence.

Only God knew of our pain on those particular days. Sandy's words revealed once again that God was holding us tightly in His grip as we faced each day without the physical presence of our son. Thousands of miles away in Canada, Sandy obeyed the prompting of the Spirit, and through her obedience God reminded us that we were neither abandoned by Him nor insignificant in His eyes. Coincidence? No.

Since only God could have made known to her our needs, I considered her words a message of hope, confidence, and courage from Him. Sandy heard the Spirit's prompting, and I thank God she listened. Did she take away our pain? No. But she helped us bear the burden.

The Prayer Mandate

God commands us to "pray continually" (1 Thessalonians 5:17). No child of God is exempt. Through prayer we encourage other believers. Biblical encouragement and prayer are like Siamese twins. The practice of prayer results in free-flowing biblical encouragement. G. Campbell Morgan illustrates this with a dramatic story.

> There are saints of God who for long, long years have been shut off from all the activities of the Church, and even from the worship of the sanctuary, but who, nevertheless, have continued to labour together in prayer with the whole fellowship of the saints. There comes to me the thought of one woman who, to my knowledge, since 1872 in this great babel of London, has been in perpetual pain, and yet in constant prayer. She is today a woman twisted and distorted by suffering, and yet exhaling the calm and strength of the secret of the Most High. In 1872 she was a bed-ridden girl in the North of London, praying that God would send revival to the Church of which she was a member, and yet into which even then she never came. She had read in the little paper called *Revival,* which subsequently became *The Christian*, the story of a work being done in Chicago among ragged children by a man called Moody. She had never seen Moody, but putting that little paper under her pillow, she began to pray, "O Lord, send this man to our Church." She had no means of

> reaching him or communicating with him. He had already visited the country in 1867, and in 1872 he started again for a short trip with no intention of doing any work. Mr. Lessey, however, the pastor of the church of which this girl was a member, met him and asked him to preach for him. He consented, and after the evening service he asked those who would decide for Christ to rise, and hundreds did so. He was surprised and imagined that his request had been misunderstood. He repeated it more clearly, and again the response was the same. Meetings were continued through the following ten days, and four hundred members were taken into the church. In telling me this story Moody said, "I wanted to know what this meant. I began making inquiries and never rested until I found a bed-ridden girl praying that God would bring me to that Church. He had heard her, and brought me over four thousand miles of land and sea in answer to her request."[4]

This encounter energized D. L. Moody to faithfully preach the gospel. A young prayer warrior took seriously the power available to her and understood that even though she was confined to a bed, prayer took her to the front lines of spiritual battlefields. As Aaron and Hur held up Moses' weary arms, this daughter of the King held up the arms of the great expositors of her day.

D. L. Moody was not alone in his belief in the supernatural power of this physically broken woman. G. Campbell Morgan continues with the story of her influence in his life:

> That girl was a member of my church when I was pastor at New Court. She is still a member, still suffering, still confined to her own room. When in 1901 I was leaving England for America I went to see her. She said to me, "I want you to reach that birthday book." I did so and turning

4 G. Campbell Morgan, *The Practice of Prayer* (New York: Revell, 1960; Grand Rapids: Baker, 1971), 125–26.

> to February 5, I saw in the handwriting I knew so well, "*D. L. Moody, Psalm 91.*" Then Marianne Adlard said to me, "He wrote that for me when he came to see me in 1872, and I prayed for him every day till he went home to God." Continuing, she said, "Now, will you write your name on your birthday page, and let me pray for you until either you or I go home." I shall never forget writing my name in that book. To me the room was full of the Presence. I have often thought of that hour in the rush of busy life, in the place of toil and strain, and even yet by God's good grace I know that Marianne Adlard is praying for me. These are the labourers of force in the fields of God. It is the heroes and heroines who are out of sight, and who labour in prayer, who make it possible for those who are in sight to do their work and win. The force of it to such as are called upon to exercise the ministry can never be measured.[5]

Paul taught the early church that prayer influenced his preaching ministry, "Pray also for me, that whenever I open my mouth, words may be given me so that I will fearlessly make known the mystery of the gospel" (Ephesians 6:19).

Is there any greater way to influence others than by offering them the treasures of our souls through prayer? Instead of focusing on the roles God does not call us to fill, it's time for more of us to influence our homes and churches through the practice of biblical prayer.

Getting Focused

1 What do you do when you don't know what to do for another person?

2 How has God directed you to meet needs that only He knew about?

5 Ibid., 126–27.

Staying Focused

Day One

1 If you do not keep a prayer journal, start one in your Blessing Book. Each day write a prayer to your Father. Start by personalizing the thanksgiving prayer in Ephesians 1:3–14.

Day Two

1 Continue in your prayer journal by personalizing Ephesians 1:15–19.
2 Using Scripture, write a prayer for a friend and send it to her.

Day Three

1 Read Ephesians 1:18 and Ephesians 3:16–17. What was Paul's motivation when he prayed for the Ephesians? Read Ephesians 6:19–20. Why did Paul want others to pray for him? Ask God to teach you how to pray for others with the same freedom. Record this prayer in your journal.

Day Four

1 Designate a page in your prayer journal for each person in your village. On one side of the page write specific needs. Record God's answers on the other side.

Day Five

1 Personalize Ephesians 1:15–19 and Ephesians 3:14–20 for someone who has special needs.

Day Six

1 Personalize Ephesians 1:15–19 and Ephesians 3:14–20 for your pastor. Write your prayer and send it to him. If you

want to study more on how to pray, read *The Practice of Prayer* by G. Campbell Morgan.

Living Focused

Offer to place a basket of pre-stamped postcards in your women's restroom. Place a small sign near the basket with the following note:

> *Has God burdened you to pray for someone today? Take a card from this basket, write an encouraging note to that person, and assure her of your prayers.*

Chapter Ten

APPLES OF GOLD IN SETTINGS OF SILVER

Carolyn's Story

When my junior high art teacher instructed our class to paint a horse, I painted a picture of a pink and purple polka-dotted pony. When my teacher held up my picture, I thought, *Oh, she's going to show the class my work and tell them this is a brilliant example of wonderful talent!*

No. She held up my picture and said, "Artists are to paint the truth. Carolyn has painted a lie. There is no such thing as a pink and purple polka-dotted pony." Then she said, "No talent here," and tore my painting in half and dropped it into the wastebasket.

Devastated, I decided that no one would ever again see my art work. I went home and became a closet painter—literally.

We had a "closet rule" in our house. Mom told us, "As long as you keep your rooms picked up, I'll never check your closets." I had a big closet off my room with white walls, and my closet became my art studio. I painted all of my favorite storybook characters on the walls—Prince Charming, Cinderella, Sleeping Beauty. On the ceiling I painted clouds and on all my wooden hangers I painted flowers.

One day my mother had friends over for lunch and I heard her say, "The dress I made for Carolyn is in her closet. Come on, HI show it to you." Running up the stairs after them, I caught up just in time to hear them "oohing and ahhing," My mother came toward me with her arms outstretched. "Why, Carolyn," she exclaimed, hugging me, "you are a painter!"

"Do you know what the Bible says about talent?" asked my mother's friend.

I didn't know, because I didn't know Jesus yet, but I was curious so I listened to her explain.

"To the one who has, more will be given in abundance," she said. "It is God who gave you the talent, but you have to pay for it by using it. Promise to do a sketch every day and God will multiply your gift."

With my mother's hug and her friend's words, a painter was born.[2]

Encouragement Principle 10

Biblical encouragement is like "apples of gold in settings of silver."

My friend Denise and I often discussed how hard it was to guard our tongues. Once when we were studying Proverbs 25:11 ("A word aptly spoken is like apples of gold in settings of silver"), I said, "Wouldn't a pin made of tiny gold apples set in silver leaves be a beautiful reminder to consider the power of our words before we speak?"

My friend remembered my comment. Several months later she presented to me a tiny gift box. Nestled inside was such a pin, designed for me at Denise's request.

Wearing it reminds me of this special young woman and of the power of words. Every wise woman I know would like to have a reputation for saying just the right encouraging words at just the right moment. A wise woman realizes that words have power to

2 Carolyn Blish is an award-winning member of the American Watercolor Society and Allied Artists of America. Reproductions of her paintings in fine art prints have received international acclaim. She is a daughter of the King who uses her creativity to display God's love and power.

either build up or tear down, and she uses her mouth to build up by inspiring those in her home, church, and other circles of influence with words of courage, spirit, or hope.

The Heart of the Matter

James tells us, "If anyone considers himself religious and yet does not keep a tight rein on his tongue, he deceives himself and his religion is worthless" (James 1:26). He continued this theme in 3:5–8:

> Likewise the tongue is a small part of the body, but it makes great boasts. Consider what a great forest is set on fire by a small spark. The tongue also is a fire, a world of evil among the parts of the body. It corrupts the whole person, sets the whole course of his life on fire, and is itself set on fire by hell. All kinds of animals, birds, reptiles and creatures of the sea are being tamed and have been tamed by man, *but no man can tame the tongue*. It is a restless evil, full of deadly poison. (Emphasis added)

In other words, if you let people talk long enough, you'll discover what kind of person they really are. This is similar to the words Jesus spoke to the Pharisees:

> You brood of vipers, how can you who are evil say anything good? For out of the overflow *of the heart* the mouth speaks. The good man brings good things out of the good stored up in him, and the evil man brings evil things out of the evil stored up in him. But I tell you that men will have to give account on the day of judgment for every careless word they have spoken. For by your words you will be acquitted, and by your words you will be condemned. (Matthew 12:34–37, emphasis added)

Words reveal our attitudes. What is in our hearts will find its way to our lips. Many times criticism and gossip are the first symptoms of conflict in homes and churches. Scripture teaches that hearts and minds not in tune with Christ produce discord:

> What causes fights and quarrels among you? Don't they come *from your desires that battle within you?* You want something but don't get it. You kill and covet, but you cannot have what you want. You quarrel and fight. You do not have, because you do not ask God. When you ask, you do not receive, because you ask with wrong motives, that you may spend what you get on your pleasures. (James 4:1–3, emphasis added)

Self-centered conflict is not a characteristic of a compassionate community; it is a black mark on the body of Christ. Throughout Scripture, God says that hearts connected to Him produce words that strengthen and heal:

> The mouth *of the righteous* is a fountain of life, but violence overwhelms the mouth *of the wicked*. (Proverbs 10:11, emphasis added)

> The tongue *of the righteous* is choice silver, but the heart *of the wicked* is of little value. (Proverbs 10:20, emphasis added)

> Reckless words pierce like a sword, but the tongue *of the wise* brings healing. (Proverbs 12:18, emphasis added)

The psalmist prayed:

> Set a guard over my mouth, O Lord; keep watch over the door of my lips. Let not my *heart be drawn to what is evil*, to take part in wicked deeds with men who are evildoers; let me not eat of their delicacies (Psalm 141:3–4, emphasis added).

In our quest to become mature encouragers, we keep returning to this issue: intimacy with Christ will drive us to connect with those in our sphere of influence to tell them who God is and what He is doing for us.

Speech that is like "apples of gold in settings of silver" starts with the heart, not the tongue. When our hearts yearn to glorify God and point others to Christ, the Holy Spirit teaches us how to encourage with words and connect with others rather than spin a protective cocoon that isolates us from them.

Taming the Tongue

Paul closed his letter to the church at Philippi with specific exhortations about godly living and then outlined the steps to follow. If our thinking is right, we will experience God's peace. Right thinking changes the desires of our hearts, and from a pure heart come words that reveal the peace of God in us and which result in peace with those around us:

> Finally, brothers, whatever is true, whatever is noble, whatever is right, whatever is pure, whatever is lovely, whatever is admirable—if anything is excellent or praiseworthy—think about such things. Whatever you have learned or received or heard from me, or seen in me—put it into practice. And the God of peace will be with you. (Philippians 4:8–9)

An Eightfold Test

Thoughts precede words, so the instructions about thinking in Philippians 4:8–9 are useful guidelines for speech as well. To avoid negative, critical speech, ask yourself these questions before speaking:

1. *Is what I am thinking true?* If I say what I am thinking, will it give an accurate impression? Be aware that if we think of something often enough, we will begin believing that it is true.

2. *Is what I am thinking noble or honorable? Noble* means that we are to move through life as though the world is the courtyard of

God. Will my words reflect an awareness of God's continual presence?

3. *Is what I am thinking right?* Are my words appropriate to say at this time? Is my urge to speak a prompt from God or a selfish desire?

4. *Is what I am thinking pure (i.e., uncontaminated by pride and selfishness)?* What is the reason for my thoughts? Is my desire to build up or tear down the other person?

5. *Is what I am thinking lovely or pleasant?* The Greek word translated *lovely* comes from the verb that means to "excite love." Will my words bring hearers into a deeper awareness of God's love?

6. *Is what I am thinking admirable?* The word *admirable* describes a very holy silence that took place just before worshipers offered sacrifices in the temple. Paul cautioned us to practice that holy silence in our hearts. Be silent for a moment and ask, *Are these words pure enough to present as a holy offering to God?*

7. *Is what I am thinking morally excellent?* Will what I am thinking motivate others to godly living?

8. *Is what I am thinking praiseworthy?* Peter used this word in 1 Peter 2:9: "But you are a chosen people, a royal priesthood, a holy nation, a people belonging to God, that you may declare the *praises* of him who called you out of darkness into his wonderful light" (emphasis added).

Praiseworthy thoughts focus on my identity in Christ and result in speech that motivates others to godly living.

Encouraging or Discouraging Words

Words build up or destroy people. There is no in-between. Compare the positive and negative powers of the tongue:

> A gentle answer turns away wrath, but a harsh word stirs up anger. (Proverbs 15:1)
>
> The tongue that brings healing is a tree of life, but a deceitful tongue crushes the spirit. (Proverbs 15:4)

> He who guards his mouth and his tongue keeps himself from calamity. (Proverbs 21:23)

> Through patience a ruler can be persuaded, and a gentle tongue can break a bone. (Proverbs 25:15)

Encouraging Words Build a Place of Safety

To assure our children that home is a safe place, we refuse to gossip about them. The family of God should have the same protective attitude for its members. Gossip is never good. It always tears down a person's reputation. Scripture details the results of gossip.[2]

> A gossip betrays a confidence, but a trustworthy woman keeps a secret. (Proverbs 11:13)

> A gossip betrays a confidence; so avoid a woman who talks too much. (Proverbs 20:19)

> Without wood a fire goes out; without gossip a quarrel dies down. As charcoal to embers and as wood to fire, so is a quarrelsome woman for kindling strife. The words of a gossip are like choice morsels; they go down to a woman's inmost parts. (Proverbs 26:20–22)

> With her mouth the godless destroys her neighbor, but through knowledge the righteous escape. (Proverbs 11:9)

> A perverse woman stirs up dissension, and a gossip separates close friends. (Proverbs 16:28)

Are you using the power of speech to build up or destroy? Lest we minimize the destructive power of gossip, note Paul's statement in Romans 1:29–32:

> They have become filled with every kind of wickedness, evil, greed and depravity. They are full of envy, murder,

2 Throughout the rest of this chapter I have replaced masculine nouns and pronouns with feminine ones in Scripture quotations.

> strife, deceit and malice. They are *gossips*, slanderers, God-haters, insolent, arrogant and boastful; they invent ways of doing evil; they disobey their parents; they are senseless, faithless, heartless, ruthless. *Although they know God's righteous decree that those who do such things deserve death, they not only continue to do these very things but also approve of those who practice them.* (Emphasis added)

These people knew better, yet they continued to gossip and to affirm others who did. Paul warned Timothy that young widows especially needed to guard against this sin:

> They get into the habit of being idle and going about from house to house. And not only do they become idlers, but also gossips and busybodies, saying things they ought not to. (1 Timothy 5:13)

Perhaps it's time to start practicing the good "gossip" described in Ephesians 4:29:

> Do not let any unwholesome talk come out of your mouths, but only what is helpful for building others up according to their needs, that it may benefit those who listen.

Ask the Holy Spirit to search your heart. If He convicts you of the sin of gossip, confess it, repent, and seek His forgiveness. Commit to replacing gossip with words that build up.

Encouraging words connect us to one another and create a safe environment for personal growth. Discouraging words tempt us to withdraw. A woman determined to connect with her world may have to practice encouraging speech, starting with the way she listens.

Apples of Gold Principles

1. *A listening heart is slow to speak.* People can listen at least three times faster than they can talk. How do you listen? While your child chatters about his day, do you think about your grocery list, what you're going to have for dinner, or an argument with your

husband? Do you interrupt people or finish their sentences? Do you pay attention just long enough to figure out what the person is saying and jump in when she takes a breath?

What nonverbal messages do you give? Do you stare past the person speaking or sneak peaks at the television? Do you continue working on your projects or do you look the person in the eye, put down your book, and turn off the television? Nonverbal messages say one of two things: "I want to understand" or "Hurry up, I have something better to do." The speaker will hear your nonverbal messages just as clearly as the verbal ones.

Do you express interest in what the other is saying by responding in a way that keeps the door of communication open or do you close doors with ridicule? Can people confide in you and feel safe or do you belittle their feelings with statements like this: "You don't really feel that way, do you?"

> Everyone should be quick to listen, *slow to speak* and slow to become angry, for woman's anger does not bring about the righteous life that God desires. (James 1:19–20, emphasis added)
>
> Reckless words pierce like a sword, but the tongue of the wise brings healing. (Proverbs 12:18)
>
> She who guards her lips guards her life, but she who speaks rashly will come to ruin. (Proverbs 13:3)
>
> A woman of knowledge uses words with restraint, and a woman of understanding is even-tempered. Even a fool is thought wise if she keeps silent, and discerning if she holds her tongue. (Proverbs 17:27–28)
>
> Do you see a woman who speaks in haste? There is more hope for a fool than for her. (Proverbs 29:20)

Don't think that your child, spouse, or friend can't tell when you are not really listening. You cheat yourself of opportunities to offer apples of gold in settings of silver when you do not listen carefully.

You will not hear the Holy Spirit guide you to ask the right questions that will open the door of conversation.

In the months after Mark's death I realized how hard and exhausting listening is. I avoided large groups because I did not have the energy to sort through their conversations. In the laboratory of grief, I realized that a listener is an encouragement treasure. Listening is a sacrifice but well worth the investment.

> Listening is midwifery, the work of someone willing to allow another to labor in pain and joy, who refuses to numb these precious things by coming too quickly to reassure or make everything right. Listening to another person enables, gently facilitates birth . . . to help another who has lost hope to come to light through the process.[3]

Ask God to make you a midwife of encouragement by teaching you to be a good listener.

2. *A listening heart produces sensitive speech*. Much relational and church conflict would dissipate if we would learn to respond rather than react to information and to refuse to judge a situation after hearing only one side of a story.

> She who answers before listening, that is her folly and her shame. (Proverbs 18:13)

> The first to present his case seems right, till another comes forward and questions him. (Proverbs 18:17)

I cannot number the times I have gotten into trouble because I reacted emotionally to one side of a story. Considering all the times my children drew me into their battles by telling a tale of woe that highlighted only their good behavior, you would think I would have learned. Although I am better at withholding judgment now, I still have to choose to think, "Is what I am hearing (and thus thinking) really true, or is there another side that will shed light

3 Marlee Alex, "An Open Window," *Virtue* (May/June 1994), 4.

on the facts I have?" Wise women listen carefully and draw no conclusions until they hear all the facts.

We can talk about good things and still be talking too much if we speak words that are motivated by selfishness rather than a desire for the good of the hearer. The following entry from the journal of Carole Mayhall forced me to examine my own motives for much of my talking:

I did it again, Lord,
And I'm sorry.
You have convicted me before
about "name-dropping,"
"place-dropping,"
"knowledge-dropping."
That wasn't the problem this time, Lord.
In sharing around the table
with a small group of dear Christians,
I realized afterward
there was an inner desire
to impress.
Oh, I didn't say anything I didn't mean.
We shared about You, Lord,
and that was good.
But somewhere in my being,
instead of sharing from an
overflowing heart,
I seemed to be sharing out
of a need to impress by my
"overflowing heart."
Forgive me, Lord!
Help me to keep silent
until You tell me to speak.[4]

---

4 Carole Mayhall, *Words That Hurt, Words That Heal* (Colorado Springs: NavPress, 1986), 78–79.

To assess the spiritual health of your heart, check your words. Do they serve yourself or others? Do they scream to get the spotlight focused on you, or do they focus the spotlight on the needs of others? Do they interrupt when others are speaking or encourage others to speak?

As you listen, think, *What words can I use to help this person grow in Christ?* Ask the Holy Spirit to fit your words to the personality of the person and the situation.

3. *A listening heart affirms others with words.* Colossians 4:6 reminds us that encouraging words should be the norm for the child of God:

> Let your conversation be *always* full of grace, seasoned with salt, so that you may know how to answer everyone. (Emphasis added)

People on salt-free diets complain about how bland food is. Eating loses some of its enjoyment. Is talking with you like being on a salt-free diet: bland and boring? Or is your life in Christ so vibrant and exciting that you have interesting things to say? Are hope, courage, and confidence the salt of your conversation? Do your words enhance the flavor of truth and make it pleasant to taste? Or are your words biting and bitter, making truth distasteful?

Use words to encourage, encourage, encourage!

4. *A listening heart accepts correction graciously.* Perhaps the most difficult thing in all the world to listen to is criticism. But Scripture is clear that wise women accept rebuke, acknowledge wrongdoing, heed correction, and grow even wiser for having listened without defensiveness and for correcting their behavior without resentment.

> The wise in heart accept commands but a chattering fool comes to ruin. (Proverbs 10:8)
>
> The way of a fool seems right to her, but a wise woman listens to advice. A fool shows her annoyance at once, but a prudent woman overlooks an insult. (Proverbs 12:15–16)

> Pride only breeds quarrels, but wisdom is found in those who take advice. (Proverbs 13:10)
>
> A fool spurns her father's discipline, but whoever heeds correction shows prudence. (Proverbs 15:5)
>
> She who listens to a life-giving rebuke will be at home among the wise. She who ignores discipline despises herself, but whoever heeds correction gains understanding. (Proverbs 15:31–32)
>
> Wounds from a friend can be trusted, but an enemy multiplies kisses. (Proverbs 27:6)
>
> A woman who remains stiff-necked after many rebukes will suddenly be destroyed—without remedy. (Proverbs 29:1)

5. *A listening heart exhorts others gently*. To exhort means "to incite by argument or advice: urge strongly; to give warnings or advice: make urgent appeals."[5]

Some believers seem to think that exhortation requires them to take on the role of Holy Spirit with friends and family members. Not so. As biblical exhorters we are neither to condemn nor to convict; we are to advise, warn, and strongly urge fellow believers to pursue godliness when they stray in their thinking or behavior:

> And with many other words John exhorted the people and preached the good news to them. (Luke 3:18)
>
> Do not rebuke an older man harshly, but exhort him as if he were your father. (1 Timothy 5:1)
>
> Brothers, I urge you to bear with my word of exhortation, for I have written you only a short letter. (Hebrews 13:22)

5 *Merriam Webster's Collegiate Dictionary*, 10th ed. (Springfield, Mass: Merriam-Webster, Inc.), 1993.

The purpose of encouragement is to help others mature in Christ, to make our homes and churches into places where believers grow and flourish and where unbelievers see Christ.

Exhortation is not easy. It requires thoughtful prayer and planning, and it always involves a risk:

> Do not rebuke a mocker or she will hate you; rebuke a wise woman and she will love you. Instruct a wise woman and she will be wiser still; teach a righteous woman and she will add to her learning. (Proverbs 9:8–9)

However, it also has the potential for great reward:

> Like an earring of gold or an ornament of fine gold is a wise woman's rebuke to a listening ear. (Proverbs 25:12)

Encouragement may at times need to be in the form of exhortation or correcting. Keep in mind, however, that the purpose of all exhortation, like that of encouragment, is to build up, not tear down. If you are eager to exhort a person, you probably are not the one God is calling to do the job. If there is any hint that your motive is to judge rather than to restore, don't get involved. Attempt exhortation only when God's leading is clear.

Steps of Biblical Exhortation

1. Submit your own heart to God's exhortation. Before attempting to restore someone else, make sure you are in a right relationship with God:

> Brothers, if someone is caught in a sin, you who are spiritual should restore him gently. *But watch yourself, or you also may be tempted.* Carry each other's burdens, and in this way you will fulfill the law of Christ. *Each one should test his own acts.* Then he can take pride in himself, without comparing himself to somebody else, for each one should carry his own load. (Galatians 6:1–5, emphasis added)

Throughout the process of exhortation, ask these two questions: Have I committed this action to the Lord? Am I certain that this is what He wants me to do?

2. *Evaluate your relationship with the person.* The word *brother* in this passage (also in Hebrews 13:22) implies that a relationship is already in place. Have you been an encourager in this person's life? Have you proven your love to her? Are you going to her as a loving sister, knowing that the best thing she can do is confess her sin and receive mercy? Or are you going as a critic who wants to have the pleasure of seeing her squirm? In other words, are you going as a loving friend or as an enemy disguised as a friend? "Wounds from a friend can be trusted, but an enemy multiplies kisses" (Proverbs 27:6).

3. *Get the facts.* How many times have you listened to one side of a story and pounced on the supposed offender before hearing his or her side? Getting the facts before drawing a conclusion shows all parties that you believe the best about them. They will know you are trustworthy.

Judgment without a fair hearing is painful, as I have learned through severe church conflict. Whenever I am tempted to judge quickly, I ask, "Do I want to treat someone the same way I was treated or do I want to give the benefit of the doubt?" Proverbs 18:13 warns, "She who answers before listening, that is her folly and her shame."

4. *Evaluate the facts.* Are you certain that the questionable behavior is sin that needs to be confessed and forsaken? Be certain that the behavior is not a mistake that needs to be covered or a difference of opinion that needs to be ignored. Proverbs 17:9 tells us, "She who covers over an offense provokes love." If the behavior is indeed sin, proceed to step 5. If, however, the woman has simply made a mistake and knows it, there is no reason to point it out to her and the rest of the church or community. Let her learn from the mistake and get on with her life. Also, if she has done something that you don't like but which you cannot honestly classify as sinful, let it rest. Matters of personal preference (e.g., clothes,

music, and lifestyle) are often mistaken for matters of righteousness, and these preferences are frequently the root of church conflict. God's Word is our only trustworthy guide.

5. *Wait on the Holy Spirit.* Let the Holy Spirit prepare the person to hear the message. While waiting for God's timing, plan your words. Proverbs 25:15 says, "Through patience a ruler can be persuaded." Timing and wording are essential. Remember how Esther in the Old Testament waited for the right moment to expose the planned slaughter of the Jews.

6. *Stick to the issue at hand.* Don't allow the person to take you down a rabbit trail that has little to do with the issue. Keep a gentle voice. Don't lose control of your temper. When you are confronting someone about sin, she may be defensive and want to point out your sin. If that happens ask, "Why didn't you approach me with this problem when it happened? If you have a problem with me, I want to hear about it, but that is not the issue at hand." "A gentle tongue can break a bone" (Proverbs 25:15).

7. *Remember the purpose of exhortation.* The purpose of exhortation is to guide and restore, not judge or condemn. God-centeredness is essential. The issue is not the sin between your sister and you but between God and her.

> She who listens to a life-giving rebuke will be at home among the wise. She who ignores discipline despises herself, but whoever heeds correction gains understanding. (Proverbs 15:31–32)

8. *Receive rebuke graciously.* If you are on the receiving end of exhortation, your response should be the same as that of the psalmist:

> Let a righteous woman strike me—it is a kindness; let her rebuke me—it is oil on my head. My head will not refuse it. (Psalm 141:5)

The woman best equipped to offer exhortation is the one who humbly welcomes it in her own life.

May we all relentlessly pursue words aptly spoken, words like apples of gold in settings of silver.

Getting Focused

1 What recent events have made you think that your body came with the instruction: "Open mouth, insert foot"?
2 Do you need to repent of gossip?
3 What are the most encouraging words anyone has ever spoken to you?

Living Focused

Day One

1 Read Philippians 4:4–9. What does Paul exhort the Philippians to think about? What result should their thoughts have on their lives?

Day Two

1 Reread Philippians 4:4–9. Identify an area in your life where your thoughts are anxious. Apply the medication of this passage to that area by asking yourself, Is what I am thinking true, noble, right, pure, etcetera. If your answer is no to any of these, seek forgiveness for your wrong thoughts and choose to think biblically.

Day Three

1 To think according to Philippians 4:4–9, we must be careful listeners. Reread Marlee Alex's quote on page 169. How is listening similar to being a midwife?
2 Ask God to make you a biblical listener.

Day Four

1 Read James 1:26. How important are our words? Read James 3:1–8. What makes the tongue so hard to control? If we have difficulty controlling our tongues, what steps

should we take to ensure that our words are "apples of gold in settings of silver"?

Day Five

1 Read Proverbs 16:28 and Romans 1:29–32. Paul lists gossip as a result of wicked and depraved hearts. Why? Read Proverbs 26:22. Why is it hard to resist gossip?

Day Six

1 Read Proverbs 11:9 and 26:20–21. Why must we resist gossip? Why must we avoid gossips (Proverb 20:19; 11:13; 16:28)? Remember, a person who gossips *to* you will gossip *about* you.

Living Focused

Be a listener today. Ask God to stop you each time you are ready to speak before thinking. Purposefully initiate a conversation with a friend or family member with the goal of listening intently without interrupting or offering quick responses.

Chapter Eleven

TREASURES IN THE WILDERNESS OF SUFFERING

Jane Anne's Story

A phone call in the middle of the night started me on a journey I did not want to take. Adrenaline pumped my body into action as I threw on my clothes, resisting what I could not avoid or deny. Rushing out the door, I pleaded with my husband, "Tell me what to say! I don't know how to help her! You have to tell me what to say!"

But he couldn't. He could only promise to pray that God would answer my plea. Sobbing and yelling expressions of disbelief to God as I raced to the hospital, I fought two conflicting desires—to be with my sister because she needed me and to stay away because there was nothing I could do to help her. I couldn't even pray for healing—her son was dead—taken away instantly in a car accident.

We had always been there for each other, but this was way beyond me. Death was never an easy subject for us—in fact it wasn't a subject at all in our family. Mother didn't even go to funerals. How could I possibly be of help in such foreign territory? Yet how could I not respond to her pain?

Over the next weeks, months, and years as I went to her home, I felt as if I was stepping into another world—a world where pain ruled and darkness shadowed every bit of life. Even two years later, on the anniversary of that awful night, I felt the familiar dread. Driving to her house with tears streaming down my face, I sobbed, "Why am I going? I can't do anything to change what has happened, and it hurts just to be there." But I went. Many times I went. I listened. I cried. And I prayed, begging God for mercy.

What happened when I stepped into my sister's pain was change—change in me. In that home filled with grief was the presence of the Provider, the Comforter, the God of Peace. Pain often prevented her from realizing His presence, but I could see the clear path He was making through her suffering. As she shared her broken heart with me, I also received the treasures He was giving to her. Watching Him work shaped and strengthened my faith. She was so weak that His strength barely sustained her, but from my position it was awesome and marvelous. We were on holy ground in this journey. God would do His part in the healing process, and I had a front-row seat. He might even use me in that process. I felt honored to help bear the heaviness of her burden. I was learning so much about death and life. I would never be the same.

Was I adequate for the task of ministering to her? Definitely not. Time and time again I felt totally incapable of dealing with her needs. Most of the time, though, I was asking more of myself than she was expecting of me. All she wanted was my love and my presence along her journey through the darkness. That usually meant just listening to what she was feeling and thinking. But just listening was excruciating, and not having answers was maddening.

Throughout my tears and frustration God led me to places I had never been and showed me things I never would have seen. My spiritual life has depth I had never experienced. I know better who I am because I know better who God is. The reality of death has brought God closer than ever. I see Him in everything now. I have confidence that He will do what I cannot do, and I know that His ways are beyond me. How grateful I am that He chose me to be the vessel from which He poured out His love to her. Little did I know on that life-changing night that the treasures found in darkness, which God was planning for her, would be mine too.

Encouragement Principle 11

God gives treasures of comfort in the wilderness of crisis and loss.

Scripture describes hell as a place of loneliness, weeping, wailing, darkness, and separation from God, and that is where I thought I must be.

When the phone rang at midnight, I expected to hear my son say, "Hey, Mom, it's me. I'm on my way home from Kelly's." But instead I heard, "Mrs. Betters, this is the Christiana Hospital. Your son Mark has been in a car accident. You need to come."

"Is he okay?" I asked.

Instead of saying, "He'll be fine," she hesitated, then replied, "He's in critical condition."

As we raced past the unrecognizable wreckage at the accident scene, we realized that our son might not have survived. When we reached the hospital, the nurse took us toward the room on the left—the place where they took family members to inform them of a death.

"I'm a pastor. I know the routine," my husband said to her. "Is my son dead?" Instead of shaking her head no to his question, she nodded yes. Instead of meekly surrendering to this horrific interruption in my life, I screamed, "No, no, no!" while pounding on my husband's chest. Thus began our descent into the valley of the shadow of death.

Later that evening, the wails of our other two young adult sons, the emptiness in my daughter's eyes, the gaping, raw grief lining my husband's face, and my own longing for Mark convinced me that surely I must be in hell. And to be present in our home must have felt like being there as well. Although surrounded by loving friends and family, we felt indescribable loneliness and abandonment by God.

How often we had stood on the precipice of this valley, peering into the darkness as it swallowed up friends, terrified by what we could not see. How many times we had heard of others who received the phone call every parent dreads, always praying that God would exempt us from this terror.

When it was someone else's suffering, I could go back to the safety of my home when the burden became too great. I could stay at the edge. But this time the tentacles of death grabbed me and pulled me down the slippery, slimy slope into a seemingly bottomless abyss.

I had tried hard to understand the deep sorrow of death, but I had never come close, and suddenly I understood why the Bible calls death the greatest enemy. I was helpless to defend myself against it.

I realize this is not easy to read. It is not easy to write. But death is as real as life, and ignoring it does not change it. We will all find time to die, and death will interrupt the lives of people we know and love. What will be our response? Grief is not a spectator sport; it demands involvement. The Bible commands us to join others in their suffering:

> Weep with those who weep. (Romans 12:15 NKJV)

> Remember those in prison as if you were their fellow prisoners, and those who are mistreated as if you yourselves were suffering. (Hebrews 13:3)

In the two following passages, God connects spiritual maturity with the ministry of comfort:

> Carry each other's burdens, and in this way you will fulfill the law of Christ. (Galatians 6:2)

> Religion that God our Father accepts as pure and faultless is this: to look after orphans and widows in their distress and to keep oneself from being polluted by the world. (James 1:27)

There are burdens only God can lift, but He expects the members of His body to use their individual gifts to create an environment of healing. Comfort is a corporate ministry.

Two years after Mark's death, the father of one of his friends wept and said, "Your pain is so profound. Praying and sending cards seems so insignificant. Isn't there more I can do?"

Many others expressed the same frustration. Profound pain seems to call for profound action. But God takes the small acts of many individuals and blends them into a healing balm.

A diagnosis of cancer sent me to the hospital for chemotherapy every four weeks for six months. For four days I watched six different solutions drip into my veins. By itself, each was insignificant, my doctor explained, but used together, they might conquer the disease. Each helped the other do its job.

This is much like the working of the body of Christ. Various passages describe the gifts God gives to His people (Romans 12:6–8; 1 Corinthians 7:7, 12:4–11). Peter challenges us:

> Each one should use whatever gift he has received to serve others, faithfully administering God's grace in its various forms. If anyone speaks, he should do it as one speaking the very words of God. If anyone serves, he should do it with the strength God provides, so that in all things God may be praised through Jesus Christ. To him be the glory and the power forever and ever. Amen. (1 Peter 4:10–11)

In the weeks and months following Mark's death, I learned how God uses seemingly small acts to make a big difference. My friend Sharon Kraemer learned this truth while undergoing treatment for an aggressive cancer and expressed it in this letter of thanksgiving:

> The outpouring of love from the body of Christ was thrilling and so encouraging. People showed their love and concern in so many different ways: cards and letters, flowers, phone calls, prepared food, house-cleaning, errands, chauffeuring to radiation treatments, lovely presents, and visits

> for fellowship. One thing I have learned from this time is that nothing done for a person going through a hard period is too "small" or insignificant to count. Every expression of interest and affection is heartwarming. These kindnesses and the prayer support reminded me of a verse in 1 Samuel 23: "Jonathan helped David find strength in God." What a wonderful definition of a friend's most important role. (August 29, 1995)

When we see our role as that of helping our friends find strength in God, rather than of making everything right for them again, we are free to let God use our service to draw to Himself those who hurt.

The depth of our relationship to the hurting person will help define our involvement, but it will never excuse us from being involved. Remember Deborah's disappointment in the tribes that refused to respond. She expected them at least to be part of a support network. She expected some contribution from each one.

The Old Testament book of Ruth is a picture of God's care for a small family during the roller-coaster rebellion of the Israelites in the time of the Judges.

Ruth's responses to Naomi teach us how to minister in the deep, dark chasms of grief. She made a covenant to care, and she never broke it. Her encouragement flowed from a surrendered heart, and her willingness to take risks made her sensitive to Naomi's real needs, which she humbled herself to meet. Ruth did not consider blessing an innate right, as shown by her willingness to work and her gratefulness to Boaz.

How grateful I am for the Ruths who followed me into the valley of the shadow of death, holding my hand, whispering, "In the name of Christ, don't be afraid. I'll go with you."

As I hold up some gems from my treasure chest, examine each one and see if there is one that you can offer a hurting friend. Each act of encouragement is a beautiful gem, but it becomes even more beautiful when placed in a setting with others.

The Surrendered Heart

The story at the beginning of this chapter describes the surrendered heart of my younger sister, Jane Anne, who became my Ruth. Just as Ruth wept with Naomi, Jane Anne wept with me. As Ruth clung to Naomi, Jane Anne clung to me, calling every day for months. Perhaps her greatest gift was that she constantly pointed me toward trust in God, telling me that even though I felt completely helpless and weak, she saw His strength permeating my life.

I did not want my sister to experience my horrific pain or see my ugliness, but she was surrendered to God, and God directed her to meet my need.

A surrendered heart does not resent interruption. Jane Anne could have excused herself from entering the wilderness of my sorrow because her family, on the day of Mark's death, adopted a beautiful little girl. Surely anyone would understand her need to focus on this child and enjoy her family. Instead, she accepted the interruption in my life as an interruption in her own. When I consider what she had to listen to—the animal-like cries of longing for my child, the rage against God, the sense of betrayal and broken dreams—I know she had to deliberately surrender her heart to our just and loving God.

A surrendered heart does not become defensive. Everything I said in the months following Mark's death challenged my sister to examine her own faith and relationship to God. But she never argued with me. She knew when to speak and when to be quiet. She listened for hours as I attempted to make sense out of my life. I said the same things again and again. Yet she never was impatient. I am sure my words often shocked her, but she never acted shocked.

The Risk-taking Heart

Boaz described the risks that Ruth took to assist Naomi. He said, in effect, "I've been told all about what you have done for your mother-in-law since the death of your husband—how you left your father and mother and your homeland and came to live with a people you did not know before."

What a picture. Since Ruth herself had lost her husband, no one would have expected her to comfort her mother-in-law; she could have left Naomi alone in her sorrow. Instead, she made herself vulnerable, leaving home to travel to a foreign land where she knew no one.

A risk-taking heart travels willingly into the foreign land of sorrow. Jane Anne soon realized that Mark's death had catapulted me to a place outside the boundaries of anything familiar and that she could not rely on her own instincts or knowledge to help me find my way back. She would have to do things that didn't come naturally. A former nurse, she wrote the following analogy to describe what she finally had to do to minister to us effectively:

> I donned the unbecoming yellow paper gown and cap and put on my rubber gloves and mask as I prepared to enter the patient's room. The effects of her disease were repulsive, and I avoided the room until her needs required my attention. Raw, open sores penetrated to the bone. Involuntary nervous responses resulted in embarrassing outbursts of unpredictable emotions. Pain permeated the room, giving a suffocating feeling to anyone who entered. The windows and glass door mocked the patient, allowing her to see a world she could not join. This patient was incapable of caring for herself in any way.
>
> Isolation always seemed ironic to me. In other cases, we put on sterile gloves to protect the patient from our germs, but isolation cases required full garb to protect us from the patient's disease. It was always risky to treat these patients. Why take it? I experienced a strange phenomenon when I chose to take that risk. Somehow I felt more alive to be in touch with such intense pain. I felt real. Of course, I took precautions and could always take off my protective layer and go back into the routine life that my patient longed to experience once again.
>
> This patient, though drenched with disease, had a strange

pull on me. I was always glad, after I began to care for her, that I could be the one to help. Once I was there, I wondered why I avoided that room so much. Perhaps it was not knowing what state I would find her in that caused my apprehension.

The key to the treatment was convincing the patient that she would get better (though no one would blame her for not believing it). All the research showed that recovery required patient confidence that it would happen. This confidence would enable the patient to participate in her treatment, speeding the healing process. I needed to give her hope.

I went into the sick room once again and began the treatment. Very little healing had taken place, and I could see that the disease was progressing. As I went about my care for the patient, trying to convince her with words that she would recover, the cumbersome isolation garb hampered me. The patient was suffering because of my inability to fully function, and she looked at me with frustration in her eyes. I was causing more pain!

For a moment I stopped, our eyes met, and I finally realized what she could not express. No, she would not ask me to put myself at risk, but she wouldn't believe my encouraging words either. I stared beyond her eyes as time stood still. Then, without a word, I removed the gloves, mask, and cumbersome paper gown. For the first time a glimmer of hope appeared in her eyes. At that moment we both began to believe that her disease—grief—would be conquered.

A risk-taking heart is willing to face the difficult questions of life. Sometimes we refuse to step into another person's pain because doing so forces us to face our own mortality and question our own beliefs. We do not want to upset our Disney-like lives.

Job's losses, as recorded in the Old Testament book bearing his name, challenged the belief system of his friends. For seven days they sat silently with him. What a gift! But then they felt compelled to come up with an explanation for Job's suffering.

Why was this so important to them? Because Job's pain challenged their faith. His losses, they concluded, must be his fault because such extreme suffering did not fit their understanding of a just God. They wanted to believe that they could control their destiny (i.e., control God) by behaving properly. It was important, therefore, that Job be made responsibile for his own calamity, otherwise they would have to face the fact that they were powerless to keep such tragedy from striking them. Job's circumstances challenged everything they wanted to believe about God, and that challenge frightened them.

May Job's words describing his friends not be said of us:

> A despairing man should have the devotion of his friends, even though he forsakes the fear of the Almighty. But my brothers are as undependable as intermittent streams, as the streams that overflow when darkened by thawing ice and swollen with melting snow, but that cease to flow in the dry season, and in the heat vanish from their channels. (Job 6:14–17)

The Sensitive Heart

Ruth was sensitive to Naomi's real needs. Today we would say she "read between the lines" of Naomi's exhortations. When Naomi told her daughters-in-law to go back to what they knew, Ruth knew that Naomi needed a companion in her grief. And when they arrived back in Naomi's homeland and Naomi told the Jewish women that she left full and came back empty, Ruth did not chastise her by saying, "Where's your gratitude? Don't I count for anything? If you're empty, what am I? How about showing some appreciation for my sacrifice?"

A sensitive heart is willing to feel pain. Ministering to those who grieve requires a thick skin and sensitivity that only the Holy Spirit can give. To minister to a grieving person requires a willingness to take an emotional punch.

Several days after Mark's death, our friend Emil hugged Chuck, who cried, "I just want to hit somebody. I'm so filled with rage!" Emil stuck his chest out, grabbed Chuck's fists and yelled, "Hit me, hit me, hit me!" Chuck refused and Emil cried, "I mean it, hit me, hit me. Do whatever it takes for me to help you."

That scene is precious to me because it showed how much Emil wanted to carry some of Chuck's pain.

One reason we refuse to crawl into the pit with a grieving friend is because we take personally their attempts to relieve their pain. Grief can change a person's personality, and friends are often frightened when grieving people start acting like strangers.

There must have been times when Naomi's emotional outbursts shook Ruth's confidence, but she did not take them personally and never wavered in her devotion.

Ruth wanted to carry some of her mother-in-law's pain, even though she could be hurt in the process.

A sensitive heart obeys the Holy Spirit. Jesus expected His disciples to risk loving others the way He loved them. To equip them for this task, He promised that the Holy Spirit would accompany them into this unknown territory. Remember that promise as you move into the uncomfortable, unfamiliar world of sorrow.

God often used Holy Spirit-inspired encouragement to meet my needs. Each act connected to all the others in a supernatural way, pointing me to the faithfulness of God.

One day I was feeling unusually lonely for Mark, and I asked God for special insight from His word to sustain me. Instead of giving me a special verse, He gave me a letter from a stranger who shared her hope in Christ and told about the healing I could expect. She had lost her son in a car accident five years earlier, and she had learned about my story through our denomination. For about two hours I felt almost normal. Why? Because her letter showed me that before I had even cried out to God, He had sent His answer. I thank God that she responded to the Holy Spirit and reached out to soothe my pain.

Another day I cried, "Lord, I'm Mark's mother. Wasn't I doing a good enough job? I should be taking care of him." That very day I received a note from a friend reminding me of conversations we had had about our children and how deeply I had impressed her with my love for our teenagers. She remembered these conversations when she heard about Mark's death. How did she know that I would need to be assured that I had indeed loved and enjoyed my son while exhorting other mothers to do the same with their children? She was sensitive to the prompting of the Holy Spirit.

One morning uncontrollable rage racked my soul. Unaware of my specific anguish, a friend called to say that she and her husband had felt as though something heavy lifted as they prayed for us that morning.

At that moment, I felt no victory. But later I realized that the Holy Spirit had moved friends to pray for me and hold up my weak arms when I could not believe in the grace of God or His love. Like Aaron and Hur who held up the arms of Moses, our friends held up our spiritual arms when we could not do so for ourselves. How precious are those who said, "We are trusting God for you."

A sensitive heart knows the power of prayer. One faithful prayer warrior still calls to tell me when God gives her a special burden to pray for me. God moved other prayer warriors who did not sleep in the days following Mark's death. In their wakefulness, they petitioned God to comfort us throughout the night, and we slept as though we were drugged.

A sensitive heart is not ashamed to cry. One Sunday I was crying even before I got out of bed, and I knew I would have a hard time at church. I considered staying home, but then thought, *If I can't cry at church, where can I cry?* I thank God for a body of believers that weeps with those who weep.

Young people seem especially gifted with such sensitivity. Mark's fellow students recorded their special memories of him and were unafraid to enter our pain. Teenage boys initiated hugs after I told them that hugging them was like hugging a part of Mark. Mark's fellow varsity basketball players sobbed openly as they wrapped their arms around us.

A sensitive heart gives permission to grieve, knowing it is God's path to healing. Marilyn Heavilin, author and speaker, has lost three sons. In a day of deep despair shortly after Mark's death I told her how hard it was for me to trust God. She replied, "One day when you have worked through all your questions and emotions, you will have a deeper awareness and understanding of the love of God." She urged me to lean into the pain and to know that God could handle all of my questions as He held me tightly in His grip. Her words freed me to grieve honestly.

Each card and personal note was a link to our heavenly Father. Cards with handwritten verses and notes were especially meaningful. Grief-stricken people hang on to every word but do not have the energy to look up Bible verses. Notes detailing memories of our son were especially meaningful. One friend told me about a short conversation she had with Mark in the church hallway, another about how he played with her little boy, another of how she loved to watch him play the drums. Another friend, realizing how difficult it was for me to be in church, hugged me and whispered, "I miss him, too."

How precious it was to know that others missed him too.

Some friends sent us pictures of Mark. Yes, they brought tears, but they were cleansing tears. Others risked mentioning Mark's name. They believed us when we insisted that it did not create unnecessary pain. Memories of Mark filter every thought we have. We yearn to talk about him. The tears are already there, and we are grateful for sensitive hearts that do not act as though he never existed.

A sensitive heart is willing to exhort. From the moment she learned of Mark's death, one special friend took over our household, organizing and directing the gifts of other believers to meet our practical needs. She called me regularly and gently insisted that she knew my public facade of strength was hiding a shattered heart. Her unconditional love was a safe haven for me when, months later in a moment of despair, I cried that I did not believe God could help me. She said, "Sharon, God does not lie. He promised to meet your need and He is going to do it. Believe Him. We will get through this."

Her exhortation gave me the strength to choose to believe God's promises. Implied in her words, "We will get through this," was the promise that she would stay in my pain for as long as it took. She kept her word by calling frequently and offering to take walks. One Saturday we walked for an hour and a half, and she listened while I talked. Just talking helped me sort through my feelings.

If we are on good terms with God, we need not worry about what to say or do. He will make it clear. In *A Silver Pen for Cloudy Days*, author Susan Lenzkes shows the importance of responding to needs without asking permission:

> Friendship gives license to show up at the door of need without asking, "When would you like me to come?" or "What would you like me to do?" Nor does friendship call out, "Just let me know if you need anything."
>
> Practiced friendship whispers, "I'll be there" and promptly steps through the door with sensitivity, respect, and understanding. But what about honoring the right to invite? Those who wait for parchment invitations wait long. Need rarely throws a party—rarely even has a voice.
>
> Yet need has its own needs. It needs protection from strangers tromping in with work boots and good intentions. It needs relief from acquaintances wearing the spiked heels of advice and pat answers. Need waits with longing for the familiar entrance of dear ones who pad barefoot through the soul on ordinary days. [1]

If you have a hurting friend, don't avoid her pain. Doing nothing makes her burden heavier. She waits with longing for your familiar smile that says, "You will get well."

A sensitive heart does not say . . .

I understand.

Call me if you need me.

---

1 Susan L. Lenzkes, *A Silver Pen for Cloudy Days*, excerpted in *The Women's Devotional Bible* (Grand Rapids: Zondervan, 1987), 681.

You can have more children, get married again, fill your life with other things, etc.

I don't know what to do. (And then prove it by doing nothing.)

God needed him more than you.

God must really love you to put you through this.

You have to get on with your life.

Don't cry.

Be strong!

A sensitive heart does not . . .

Try to be always cheerful.

Try to explain why.

Think her grieving friend is crazy.

Compare losses.

A sensitive heart will say . . .

I love you.

I'm so sorry this has happened.

Nothing. (But give lots of hugs and shed lots of tears.)

I'll be in touch (and follows through).

I'm praying (and does).

A sensitive heart will . . .

Listen.

Allow her friend to express all emotions and not interject judgmental comments, especially in the beginning.

Read books that teach her how to help.

Keep visits short, unless the hurting friend insists she stay longer.

Discern when her friend needs to be alone, but not allow her to isolate herself completely.

Assure her friend that she is not crazy, just brokenhearted.

Offer to find more help when she senses her friend is sinking.

Acknowledge the pain.

Give permission to talk about the loss.

Stay in touch for the long haul with cards, phone calls, and special remembrances on anniversaries, birthdays, special holidays.

Ask the Holy Spirit for specific Scripture to share at the right moment and trust God to use them as a healing balm.

Offer to do menial tasks (but never disturb the possessions of a deceased person without permission—i.e., do not clean out his or her room, change the bed, etc.).

Recognize that grief is a long process.

Tolerate volatile outbursts and intense emotions.

Not expect or demand thanks.

Pray, pray, pray every time she thinks of her friend.

The Servant's Heart

Faithful friends with servant's hands not only encouraged me to keep moving but came alongside to help me do so. One special friend called every week to decide what project we would work on to get our house ready for our daughter's December wedding. She came alongside to help make decisions, paint, paper, redecorate. One day she organized a group of about ten people who did a summer's worth of yard work while others painted kitchen cabinets. They looked around, saw what needed to be done, and did it. They understood that we had no idea of what our needs were. They didn't say, "Call me if you need me." Most bereaved people will not respond to that message. It isn't that we aren't grateful. It's just that we are on emotional overload. Every bit of energy is being used for survival.

Friends stayed with us through the night of the accident and the days following. They prayed and wept with us, kept the coffee going, and made sure there was food in the house, plenty of paper goods, tissues in every room, and cold wet cloths for our faces. They kept lists of gifts, phone calls, and messages. They ironed shirts, put away clean clothes, took out the trash, watered and ran the dogs, and watered the flower beds. All without asking what we needed them to do.

Others realized that we needed to be in charge of details concerning Mark, and they brought those decisions to us rather than making them for us.

Some people prefer privacy in their grief, but for us the constant flow of friends to our home satisfied our need for a physical expression of God's love. We needed to see their tears, feel their hugs, see the agony in their faces. Beautiful flowers and plants reminded us of the beauty of our son—now serving God in heaven. Parents who had lost children stepped back into their own pain to give us hope. Friends helped clean Mark's room and were with me when I found his prayer journal—further affirmation of his walk with Christ.

Galatians tells us to bear one another's burden so that we can bear our own burdens. In the first few months of our grief, the body of Christ swept us up and carried us along—we were powerless to carry ourselves. Now, as a result of their encouragement and strength, we are beginning to bear our own burdens.

After Mark's death, I questioned the sufficiency of God to help us survive. But God, in His grace, provided members of His body who believed in His sufficiency for us when we could not believe it for ourselves.

Grief is terrifying both to those experiencing it and those who have to watch it happen. We want to make it go away, but the Bible tells us there is a time to grieve. It is a natural process that leads to healing and wholeness.

Wise encouragers know they are there to facilitate the process, not stop it. For people who are problem solvers, this is a hard assignment. An understanding of God's sovereignty equips us for this job. Although circumstances do not make sense, God does, and He will supply whatever His children need.

When we believe that God is sovereign, we will see Him everywhere, even in the darkness of death. That is why the first step of encouragement in the shadow of death is surrender to the God of all life. Each time we reflect that surrender by comforting others in His name, the body of Christ shines more brightly with the precious treasures of encouragement.

Getting Focused

1 Do you find it difficult to minister to people experiencing profound loss?

2 If yes, why do you think this is true?

Staying Focused

Day One

1 Read the book of Ruth and ponder the beauty of this love story. What character qualities of God do you see in Ruth? In Boaz?

Day Two

1 Read Ruth 1:16–17. Ruth makes a covenant with Naomi. What is a covenant? What makes this covenant so remarkable? What similarities do you see in her words and these Scriptures: Hebrews 13:5; Joshua 1:5; Deuteronomy 31:6, 8? How does Ruth's declaration display the character of God? Is there someone to whom God wants you to make a caring commitment, no matter how long the healing takes?

Day Three

1 Read Ruth 1:16–17; 2:2; 3:5. What risks did Ruth take? What risks must you take to comfort a hurting friend? Have you isolated yourself because you were "burned" by taking risks in the past? Read Ruth 1:8, 20–21. How might Naomi's words hurt Ruth? People who are hurting often hurt others. If that has happened to you, consider trying again, prayerfully asking God to direct each step.

Day Four

1 Reread the book of Ruth. Describe the love between Ruth and Naomi. Think of a friend in your life who has extended unconditional love to you. If you haven't expressed your thanks recently, write her a note or give her a small gift to remind her of your gratefulness for her friendship.

Day Five

1 Read Ruth 2:11–12. How did Ruth take care of Naomi's practical needs? List some practical ways you can serve a hurting friend.

Day Six

1 The foundation of Ruth's ministry to Naomi was a heart surrendered to God. God does not call all of us to minister equally to everyone. He directs us as we surrender to Him through time spent in His Word and in prayer. Is your heart surrendered to His direction?

Living Focused

Ask God to give you a burden for a person experiencing profound loss. Even if you are experiencing tough times, commit to ministering to this person. Your ministry might be as simple as a card with a personal note telling her that God impressed you to pray for her at a specific time. Or He may lead you to offer to clean her house, baby-sit children, chauffeur to a doctor's appointment. God may even surprise you by bringing to mind a friend whose loss occurred several years before and who appears "healed." How exciting for Him to move you to meet needs that only He could know about! There are treasures in darkness. Don't miss them by refusing to accompany those whom God is leading through a valley of shadow.

Chapter Twelve

ORDINARY PEOPLE, EXTRAORDINARY MINISTRY

Linda's Story

Life was good. Exciting challenges and busy days filled my time. As a wife of eighteen years and the mother of two daughters (ages 4 and 7), I was finally a stay-at-home mom at age 37. I loved teaching women's Bible study and being a homeroom mother.

In the spring of life, when times are good, we need to be preparing for winter. Because winter will come. During my springtime I said yes to many opportunities to be involved in the Lord's work, and I met Christians who loved me and prayed for me. They became the friends who encouraged me during my winter.

Because winter did come. The miscarriage of my first child and the death of my father did not compare to the bitter grief and uncertainty that gripped my heart when my unfaithful husband chose divorce as an escape from our marriage. The rejection, fear, and insecurity I felt were like ugly rags wrapped tightly around my heart.

The encouragement of believers brought me through many ordeals in the years that followed, and their godly counsel and support often pulled me out of despair and depression. The financial assistance of Christian friends and my church were God's answer to specific prayers. An uplifting note when I was on the brink of tears, a kind phone call, or an unexpected visit reminded me of God's love and made difficult steps of obedience easier to take. Although I was often lonely and impatient with God's timing, He kept me walking His pathway to holiness.

The practical love of my friends drew my children to the source of that love, giving me the desire of my heart—my daughters know, love, and fear the Lord.

Before my divorce I was the strong one who encouraged others. It was difficult and embarrassing to be the needy one. I never realized how much pride I had. Choosing to receive encouragement as a gift from God changed my pride into humility. Through my painful circumstances, God taught me that women who hide their feelings rarely receive the encouragement they need, so I learned to let people know the real me. I also learned that true encouragers do not judge others. My counsel to women like me is this: "God has already provided your encouragement; don't be afraid to receive it."

Encouragement Principle 12

God transforms the encouragement of ordinary people into extraordinary ministry.

The Privilege of Encouragement

When we have a clear picture of our own sinfulness and inadequacies, we may conclude that we are unfit to carry the great gospel message. But our wrong conclusions will not thwart God's purposes. For reasons we do not understand, God has chosen us to spread His message of hope and redemption. Acts 1:8 tells us we will be His witnesses.

In describing his passion for the Israelites, Paul explained how they would hear the message:

> As the Scripture says, "Anyone who trusts in him [Jesus] will never be put to shame." For there is no difference

> between Jews and Gentile—the same Lord is Lord of all and richly blesses all who call on him, for, "Everyone who calls on the name of the Lord will be saved."
>
> How, then, can they call on the one they have not believed in? And how can they believe in the one of whom they have not heard? And how can they hear without someone preaching to them? And how can they preach unless they are sent? As it is written, "How beautiful are the feet of those who bring good news!" (Romans 10:11–15)

"How beautiful are the feet of those who bring good news!" is a quotation from Isaiah 52:7:

> How beautiful on the mountains are the feet of those who bring good news, who proclaim peace, who bring good tidings, who proclaim salvation, who say to Zion, "Your God reigns!"

In biblical times, there was no CNN to take people into the battle zone via television. Instead, messengers ran from the war zones to inform anxious family members and friends of the outcome of the battles. In this passage the message is one of victory, "Your God reigns!"

That is the message biblical encouragers learn in the heat of their own battles and then proclaim to weary warriors in other war zones. Perhaps you think that you have little to offer, and that the encouragement mandate is impossible for you to obey.

Before you draw that conclusion, consider the ordinary people of Scripture whose simple obedience in everyday life resulted in the extraordinary proliferation of the gospel. The gospel flourished because they did what needed to be done, one task at a time. Do you consider yourself ordinary? God delights in using the ordinary to accomplish the extraordinary. He transforms the mundane into the majestic, the simple into the sacred.

Ordinary People, Extraordinary Ministry[1]

As I have expressed repeatedly in this book, compassion thrives when women in an intimate relationship with Christ reveal that relationship in the way they interact with others. Some New Testament women were our example:

> After this, Jesus traveled about from one town and village to another, proclaiming the good news of the kingdom of God. The Twelve were with him, and also some women who had been cured of evil spirits and disease: Mary (called Magdalene) from whom seven demons had come out; Joanna the wife of Cuza, the manager of Herod's household; Susanna; and many others. These women were helping to support them out of their own means. (Luke 8:1–3)

What motivation drove these women not only to follow Jesus and the disciples but to support them financially? They all had a story—what they were before Christ, what they became in Christ, and what hope they had because of Christ. Their support of Christ and His disciples was a sermon without words. They ran from their own private battlefields to proclaim with actions and words, "Our God reigns! The battle is won!"

No child of God is exempt from this type of preaching ministry, nor should she desire to be. Each one has a similar story.

Have you experienced salvation? If so, you have a message. Has God given you victory over pride, anger, a loose tongue? Then you have a message. Has He comforted you through trauma, illness, financial loss? You have a message. How do you present this message? By seeing all of life as an opportunity to express gratitude to God:

> And whatever you do, whether in word or deed, do it all in the name of the Lord Jesus, giving thanks to God the Father through him. (Colossians 3:17)

1 I first heard some of these ideas in a Bible study taught by my friend Joan Watson.

Doing What Needs to Be Done

There are others in Scripture who did what needed to be done. Although they were not "preachers" as we think of preachers, their service was vital in spreading the gospel. Among these servants were those who carried letters from the apostles to the churches. Each faced the temptation to hide from danger rather than expose themselves to it. But they chose to risk their own security to carry Paul's letters:

> Epaphroditus delivered Paul's letter to the Philippians (Philippians 2:25–30).
>
> Tychicus delivered Paul's letter to the Ephesians (Ephesians 6:21–22).
>
> Phoebe probably delivered Paul's letter to the church at Rome (Romans 16:1).
>
> Onesimus delivered a letter to Philemon (Philemon 12).

Paul wrote the letters of hope, exhortation, and salvation, but others delivered them. It took different parts of the body of Christ working together to accomplish God's purposes. Each task increased the unity of the believers.

Using Our Abilities to Open Doors of Communication

In Acts 9:36 we read about Tabitha, or Dorcas, who was always doing good and helping the poor. Her abilities as a seamstress gave her opportunities to express the good news of Jesus. Surely there were other seamstresses. What made Dorcas so special? Her actions revealed her intimacy with Jesus.

> All the widows stood around him [Peter], crying and showing him the robes and other clothing that Dorcas had made while she was still with them. (Acts 9:39)

Dorcas did not use her abilities for self-aggrandizement. She served the widows and others often forgotten by society. Dorcas would not receive any financial gain from such a ministry of encouragement. Yet truly the women she touched could cry out,

> How beautiful on the mountains are the feet and hands of Dorcas who brought us good news, who proclaimed peace, who brought good tidings when she brought us handmade garments, who proclaimed the salvation available through the sacrifice of Jesus, who said to us, "Your God reigns!" (Isaiah 52:7, my own amplification)

These are just a few of the ordinary people whose service God used to accomplish extraordinary ministry. God gave them the privilege of participating in the spiritual birthing and sanctification process of His church.

Redefining Preaching

God has ordained not only our salvation but also the means by which we come to know Him: the preaching of the gospel. But we must not confine preaching to Sunday mornings at 11:00. Preaching is an event in which one person proclaims God's Word of truth while another listens as the Spirit of God illumines these truths. Often the sanctuary is not a church building. It may be a kitchen table over a cup of coffee, an aerobics class, the office, grocery line, schoolroom, or countless other places where God arranges divine appointments. Every time we encourage, we preach. We never know when God will use our actions and words to ease one of His children into His family and start them on a journey toward holiness.

The Spiritual Birthline

God is a God of order, and He does not save people haphazardly. God elects, the Son atones, and the Spirit applies. Ephesians 1 makes this abundantly clear.

First, God the Father issues the decree concerning salvation:

> Paul, an apostle of Christ Jesus by the will of God, To the saints in Ephesus, the faithful in Christ Jesus: Grace and

> peace to you from God our Father and the Lord Jesus Christ. Praise be to the God and Father of our Lord Jesus Christ, who has blessed us in the heavenly realms with every spiritual blessing in Christ. For he chose us in him before the creation of the world to be holy and blameless in his sight. In love he predestined us to be adopted as his sons through Jesus Christ, in accordance with his pleasure and will—to the praise of his glorious grace, which he has freely given us in the One he loves. (Ephesians 1:1–6)

Second, the Son secures our redemption and satisfies the wrath of God:

> In him we have redemption through his blood, the forgiveness of sins, in accordance with the riches of God's grace that he lavished on us with all wisdom and understanding. And he made known to us the mystery of his will according to his good pleasure, which he purposed in Christ, to be put into effect when the times will have reached their fulfillment—to bring all things in heaven and on earth together under one head, even Christ.
>
> In him we were also chosen, having been predestined according to the plan of him who works out everything in conformity with the purpose of his will, in order that we, who were the first to hope in Christ, might be for the praise of his glory. (Ephesians 1:7–12)

Third, the Holy Spirit applies the work of salvation. In this we see the eternal brilliance of encouragement:

> And you also were included in Christ when you heard the word of truth, the gospel of your salvation. Having believed, you were marked in him with a seal, the promised Holy Spirit, who is a deposit guaranteeing our inheritance until the redemption of those who are God's possession—to the praise of his glory. (Ephesians 1:13–14)

The Birthing Process

Jesus, in comparing our spiritual birth with physical birth, illustrates the birthing process:

> Now there was a man of the Pharisees named Nicodemus, a member of the Jewish ruling council. He came to Jesus at night and said, "Rabbi, we know you are a teacher who has come from God. For no one could perform the miraculous signs you are doing if God were not with him."
>
> In reply Jesus declared, "I tell you the truth, no one can see the kingdom of God unless he is born again."
>
> "How can a man be born when he is old?" Nicodemus asked. "Surely he cannot enter a second time into his mother's womb to be born!"
>
> Jesus answered, "I tell you the truth, no one can enter the kingdom of God unless he is born of water and the Spirit. Flesh gives birth to flesh, but the Spirit gives birth to spirit. You should not be surprised at my saying, 'You must be born again.' The wind blows wherever it pleases. You hear its sound, but you cannot tell where it comes from or where it is going. So it is with everyone born of the Spirit."
>
> "How can this be?" Nicodemus asked.
>
> "You are Israel's teacher," said Jesus, "and do you not understand these things?" (John 3:1–10)

Nicodemus was quite confused when Jesus paralleled natural birth with spiritual birth:

> Just as we are physically conceived, we are spiritually conceived.
>
> Just as we are physically incubated in the womb for an appropriate time, we are spiritually incubated in the Spirit and prepared for conversion.
>
> Just as we are physically born, we are spiritually born.

The fact that babies born prematurely are unhealthy is a warning that we should not become overly zealous spiritual midwives who try to force premature spiritual birth or growth.

Elements of the Spiritual Birthline

The Bible teaches that all of us are totally depraved and without hope to save ourselves. We cannot by our good works do anything that is sufficient for salvation. There is no such thing as "inherent faith" or a "spark of deity" that is sufficient to save us. We cannot be saved apart from faith. We must choose Christ, repent of our sins, and by faith trust Christ and Christ alone for salvation. But how can this happen since we are by nature dead in sin? How can that which is dead respond to the command to repent and believe? The good news is that God has promised to regenerate sinners. He implants in the elect the ability to believe, draws them to the cross, and gives them eyes of faith to see Christ's redemptive work, repent of sin, and receive salvation.

But this process may take time. God uses a variety of people, circumstances, and events to prepare the soil to receive the seed of the gospel. Remember what Paul said:

> How, then, can they call on the one they have not believed in? And how can they believe in the one of whom they have not heard? And how can they hear without someone preaching to them? (Romans 10:14)

The visible expression of our relationship with Christ is God's witness of redemption to the world. He incubates His Word in the hearts of His elect, and He cultivates the soil so the seed of faith will one day germinate. Then, as that word takes root—day by day, moment by moment—He prepares us for glory through the sanctifying work of His Spirit. Each day we learn more about putting off the old man and putting on the new. We are renewed by God's grace and enabled by the Holy Spirit to pursue holiness and prepare for glory.

Encouragement Along the Birthline

The ministry of encouragement occurs all along this birthline. We are the midwives of encouragement, the ambassadors of the Spirit in this awesome birthing process. We preach the word of hope, not necessarily with eloquent speech, but more often in acts of encouragement empowered by the Spirit who draws to Himself the elect, saves them, and prepares them for their glorious inheritance, which He guards for them in heaven.

Anywhere along that birthline, God may use a timely word of encouragement to open the callous heart of one of His elect. We do not know the mysteries of His saving timetable for His children. We do not know where people are along the birthline. But we do know that God uses the "foolishness of preaching" to bring to completion what He ordained from the foundation of the world. It's humbling to realize that God uses the preaching of our lives to ease His children into His family.

We are more effective encouragers when we realize that each person in our circle of influence is on her own spiritual journey and that we must fashion our encouragement accordingly. For example, if I know a young woman in my church is not yet a believer, I will ask God to show me ways to point her to faith in Christ. If a Christian woman is struggling with infertility, I will ask God to use my actions and words to deepen her trust in Jesus. If a young woman tells me she wants to be more disciplined in her walk with Christ, I will look for ways to encourage the process of sanctification.

Geri's Journey Along the Birthline

When Geri's husband of twenty-three years walked out of her life, Sally and other Christian friends faithfully offered Geri the treasures of encouragement. The practice of biblical encouragement was and continues to be a key element God is using in Geri's sanctification. The loving outreach of her friends turned her eyes from her circumstances to her Savior. Geri learned that God often answers before we cry out to Him. She sometimes worked more than sixty hours a week and still did not have enough money at the end of the month to support her children. Sally and her husband, Bill, often slipped an envelope of cash into Geri's hand saying, "Someone wanted you to have this." An elderly gentleman worked on her old car to keep it running. When the car finally died, Sally's sister collected enough money from Christian friends for Geri to buy another car. One Christmas Eve church friends gave Geri two hundred dollars. "All sorts of ways to spend that money went through my mind," she said. "But when we arrived home from church the house was cold and the oil tank empty. I was grateful to find someone to fill it on Christmas Eve, but even more grateful to have the money to pay for it—one hundred and eighty dollars. God proved His love by providing for our needs before I even knew what they were."

These encouragers did not know how vital their role was in convincing Geri that God loved her. Their obedience to the encouragement mandate made them God's promise keepers. God transformed the mundane into the majestic, the simple into the sacred.

The faithful ministry of Geri's friends during her difficult circumstances taught Geri to walk with Christ. Now she regularly encourages others. In the hands of the Holy Spirit, the ministry of ordinary people brought extraordinary results.

The Privilege of Encouraging

Obedience to the encouragement mandate makes us privileged participants in the spiritual birthing process. Can you envision how God may be using you to draw someone to the foot of the cross? The question is one of obedience. Can you offer encouragement to others as an act of love and gratitude for your own redemption? Will you be a spiritual midwife?

The Ultimate Result of Encouragement

Out of the darkness that shrouded me after the deaths of Mark and Kelly came the light of God's love reflecting from the body of Christ in their gifts of encouragement. God's purpose in giving me these treasures was "so that you may know that I am the Lord, the God of Israel, who summons you by name" (Isaiah 45:3).

> I am the Lord, and there is no other; apart from me there is no God. I will strengthen you, though you have not acknowledged me, so that from the rising of the sun to the place of its setting men may know there is none besides me. I am the Lord and there is no other. (Isaiah 45:5–6)

God's purpose in encouraging me is not to make me feel "warm and fuzzy" but to draw me into intimacy with Him and to create in me a new awareness of His love for me, Sharon Betters. The purpose of the encouragement He sent my way was to turn my attention toward Him. God's messengers of encouragement to me were participants in the sanctifying process of my life.

God gave me another treasure in the darkness—a deeper eternal perspective. The deaths of Mark and Kelly unbolted me from this earth. Heaven is so much closer. Every night when I lie down to sleep, I remember, I am one day nearer to when I will see Jesus. One day closer to when I will experience the fulfillment of all of His promises. With that thought comes the realization that this world really is not my home. I am a sojourner who has work to do while I travel through it.

What impact will I have? Will my life point others toward Jesus and away from the pursuit of their own desires? Will my life say to the people in my village, "Our God reigns!"

When the Day of Resurrection comes, will I be able to say to my Father the words Jesus said to Him right before the Crucifixion: "I have brought you glory on earth by completing the work you gave me to do"? (John 17:4).

Every child of God must ask and answer these questions. God wants His children to delight in the privilege of representing Him to a wicked and needy world.

Life is fleeting. We have no guarantee of an earthly tomorrow. As we live each day, let us

> consider how we may spur one another on toward love and good deeds. Let us not give up meeting together, as some are in the habit of doing, but let us encourage one another—and all the more as you see the Day approaching. (Hebrews 10:24–25)

May we rise in His power, shine in the light of His love, and spread treasures of encouragement to everyone we meet.

Getting Focused

1. Where are you in your spiritual birthline?
2. Who influenced you to give your life to Christ?

Staying Focused

Day One

1. Consider your own spiritual journey. Write a thank-you note to someone who encouraged you to know and grow in Christ. Add the person's name to your Blessing Book.

Day Two

1. Read Acts 9:36–43. God used the actions of ordinary people to spread the gospel. What changed Dorcas from an ordinary woman into an extraordinary disciple? Why was her ministry extraordinary?
2. What specific abilities do you have that God might use to open up channels of communication with the people in your village?

Day Three

1. Read Romans 10:11–15 and Isaiah 52:7. Define preaching. How do you preach the gospel? What story can you tell about your own "battlefields" that ends with the proclamation, "Our God reigns!"? What person in your village

will benefit from hearing that story? Ask God to give you an opportunity to tell it.

Day Four

1 Read Isaiah 45:2–5. What is God's purpose in giving us treasures in the darkness? What should be our purpose when we give the treasures of encouragement?

Day Five

1 Review the needs of the people in your village. Where is each one in his or her spiritual journey? Write down one specific way you will encourage three of those people.

Day Six

1 Read Hebrews 10:19–25 one more time. May this passage become a driving force in your life!

Living Focused

Review your answers to Day Three and write a two-minute testimony describing an area of your life God has changed. Describe who you were before you grew in this area, how Jesus made a difference, and how His love influences you today. Pray that God will give you an opportunity to share your testimony with another person who has a similar struggle. Be very sensitive to His leading.

ACKNOWLEDGMENTS

By the time the second of our four children was born, Chuck, my husband and best friend, knew this book was in me. For more than twenty-seven years he has encouraged me to rise and shine wherever God places me, and it is due to his encouragement that this book exists. His wisdom sent me back to the computer for many rewrites, and when my words made no sense, his insights and observations brought clarity.

I am grateful to the body of Christ at the Glasgow Reformed Presbyterian Church (now Reach Church), and especially to the faithful members of my prayer chain, who claimed this book as their own before I even knew I could write it. They are a physical expression of God's love for our family and a model of the principles of biblical encouragement.

I am also grateful to the women whose stories appear in this book. The fingerprints of these God-sent encouragers are on every page. May they each receive great joy from knowing that they are participating with Christ in His work of grace.

Thank you to the Women's Advisory Sub-Committee of the Presbyterian Church in America who asked me to write this book and then prayed for me until its completion. A special thanks to Susan Hunt, who, when I felt completely inadequate for the task, encouraged me by expressing her confidence that God would be faithful in guiding me.

It was a joy to work with the P&R Publishing team whose commitment to doctrinal purity spurred me on in my commitment to think biblically and to encourage others to do so as well. Twenty-five years later I am even more appreciative of Bryce Craig's leadership in convincing the P&R team that *Treasures of Encourage-*

ment needed to be published. Thom Notaro, Barbara Lerch, and Julie Link seemed to know just what I was attempting to say. I am a better communicator and writer due to their giftedness. Many thanks to my new friends, Amanda Martin and Dave Almack, who oversaw the release of this twenty-fifth anniversary edition of *Treasures of Encouragement*. When I thought some deadlines might be impossible, they cheered me on, and I love the results!

Twenty-five years ago I held the first copy of this book in my hands, turning each page in amazement of how the Lord oversaw each detail. In the darkest days of my life, His light pushed through the broken places. May His faithfulness to me encourage you to think and live biblically, with confidence in His faithfulness to keep all His promises. To Him be all the glory.

Appendix A

A TREASURY OF ENCOURAGEMENT IDEAS

Use the ideas below for personal or group encouragement. For instance, ask your Bible study group to pick one idea to incorporate each week either on a personal or group level. As an individual, commit to implementing one encouragement idea each week and keep a record in your journal of your intentional act of encouragement and any response, especially when the recipient tells you your act of love came at just the right time.

1. Organize a small group to study *Treasures of Encouragement.* A leader's guide is available at www.pcabookstore.com.
2. Look for opportunities to cultivate community in the mundane moments of life. Spiritual mothering often happens more around a kitchen table than in a structured study.
3. Give a struggling friend a "joy box." Fill it with treasures of encouragement, i.e., notes, small gifts, gift card to her favorite coffee shop, and so on. (For more ideas, see chapter 1 and the leader's guide.)
4. Regularly text or call your grandchildren or children. Texting is a good way to share Scriptures and to tell them how you are praying for them individually.
5. Ask your children or grandchildren for specific ways to pray for them. Follow up with how you are praying and ask how they are doing.

6. Periodically send cards with a personal note to grandchildren or children, no matter their age. If you enjoy writing, send a monthly note to each grandchild and share your life, present and past. Handwritten letters will be saved and discovered years later as a special gift from beloved grandparents or parents.
7. Give each of your grandchildren a Joy Box in which to keep your notes and small gifts designed to help turn their hearts toward Jesus.
8. Refuse to give in to hurt if your children or grandchildren do not respond when you reach out to them. Be intentional and take responsibility for the relationships.
9. One of the best places to meet women is the church nursery. Volunteer to serve on a regular basis. Pray for the Lord to make you sensitive to the mother who needs encouragement. Bring cards to the nursery so you are prepared to write a personal note to a mom and slip it into the diaper bag.
10. Tell a struggling mother, "This, too, shall pass," and share a time when you noticed what a good parent she is. Those few words will stick in her heart for the rest of her life.
11. Pray for the Lord to connect you with a family that doesn't have grandparents nearby. Slowly but intentionally connect by speaking to the children, inviting the family for dessert or a meal, and asking how you can pray for them. If the friendship develops, offer to attend special school and sports events. Surprise the family with snacks for the ride home after church.
12. Be a surrogate grandmother to the pastor's family, especially if they are far from home. We will always be grateful for the older people in our churches who paid special attention to our young children.
13. Look for a single mom who needs extra hands on a Sunday morning. As your friendship grows, if you are able, offer to watch her children for a few hours.

14. Send notes to your pastor, church staff, or elders, letting them know that you are praying.
15. Organize several friends to prepare and deliver lunch to your church staff.
16. Are you retired? Pray about where to volunteer, especially in the context of connecting with younger women or children. Meet with your pastor or church staff member who oversees ministries to let them know you are looking for a place to use your experience. Be intentional in praying for opportunities to pass on to the next generation the love of Jesus.
17. Write a letter to each member of your family describing why you are glad he or she is a part of your life. Give a copy to them now but also file a copy with your will to be read after your death.
18. Do idea 17 for special friends.
19. Make a list of people who have hurt your feelings. Ask God to search your heart for any bitterness. As the Lord replaces your bitterness with forgiveness, consider doing something nice for each person on the list.
20. Ask a leader in a church ministry what his or her needs are—time, books, equipment, refreshments? Ask several friends to join you in meeting one of those needs.
21. Find a Scripture that describes a good quality in a younger woman, and send a copy of the verse to her along with a note of explanation and appreciation.
22. Treat a younger woman to breakfast. Ask someone who needs extra attention. If she is struggling, text encouraging Scriptures to her a few times a week.
23. Grandmothers, don't compete with the other grandparents. Be grateful for the ways they love your grandchildren, perhaps in ways you cannot. Express your gratitude for extended family.
24. When someone asks you to pray, stop and pray with them.

25. Pray about how you can come alongside your pastor's wife as an encourager.
26. Pack a basket of potato salad, sandwiches, fried chicken, and fruit for a family that's moving.
27. Deliver a bucket filled with cleaning supplies to a friend's new house or apartment. Stay and help to clean if you can.
28. Prepare a double batch of your favorite dinner and take it to a young woman. Consider single women as well as young moms.
29. Ask the Lord to connect you with an older woman who wants to invest in a younger woman.
30. Be intentional about connecting with older women in your church or neighborhood. Especially check in on older women living alone.
31. If you know a woman who is unable to drive, offer to take her shopping, out for lunch, or to a park. Offer to pick up groceries or medicine. If she is hesitant to ask for help, give her gift coupons for free grocery pickup, dinner, shopping, a walk around the neighborhood, a visit, cleaning, and so on. Ask her each week which coupon she wants to redeem.
32. Regularly connect with an older woman who must stay close to home because of physical disabilities. Make a quick visit or phone call. Does she like jigsaw puzzles? Stop by each week to put together the puzzle with her.
33. Offer to bring ingredients for a specialty dish so an older woman can show you how to make it. Such activities will create conversation opportunities.
34. Ask an older woman to go for a walk. When younger women ask me to walk with them, I pray to be sensitive to their unspoken needs.
35. When you observe an older woman extending kindness, send her a note telling her why her behavior encouraged you.

36. Ask your parents to tell your children about their childhood. Create some questions to get the conversation started.
37. Do yard work for a shut-in as a family project.
38. If you don't have grandparents nearby, get to know an older woman, and if the relationship turns into a friendship, ask her to be a stand-in grandmother.
39. Whatever ministry you are involved in, be intentionally generational in the committees or support team. Be on the lookout for retired women who may feel "thrown to the curb" and tap into their expertise.
40. Be sure the older women in your church know they are valued. Ask an older woman for her expertise about a ministry she led when she was younger.
41. Treat an older woman to lunch, and ask her to share her story. To get the conversation started, prepare questions like, Why did you pick ________ as a career? What did you like about it the most, the least? Where did you grow up, and what was the hardest part of growing up? The best? Did you attend church as a child? How was church then different than church today? What is your favorite hymn, and why? What are your favorite books? Your favorite Scripture, and why? What would you say to your twenty-year-old self?
42. Pack a picnic basket, and invite an older woman to join you and your kids at the park.
43. Invite older single women to join your family for dinner, holidays, or special events.
44. Ask a nursing home administrator for the name of a woman who has no visitors, and, with permission from the staff, start visiting her with the goal of developing a friendship. When appropriate, take your children for a quick visit. To make your children more comfortable, take a favorite children's book and suggest that your older friend read it to your children. On holidays, ask your children to share special songs and so on.

45. If your pastor is older, surprise his wife with a special luncheon prepared by the younger women in the church. Make it festive with balloons, a gift card for dinner, and so on. Ask each woman to pray for her or share how she has encouraged them.
46. Prepare extra dessert to share with a friend. Drop it off or share it together.
47. Encourage your children to stay connected to their grandparents, whether through visits, phone calls, texts, or emails. Help your parents understand the best way to connect with their grandkids. Ask the grandparents to attend special events; include dinner at your house before or after. Ask your parents to pray for specific needs.
48. Text encouragement to older women who are isolated by illness or age. Ask the pastor or deacons for suggestions of older women isolated by health issues or age. Visit with the purpose of identifying what practical needs you or a group of women could meet.
49. Organize a group of women to clean the house of an older woman who is homebound. Take your own supplies and include lunch or dinner.
50. Sit with a woman who is alone in church or at special events. Offer to meet her at the door or drive together.

The Blues Busters

Shortly after our son's death, we received surprise encouragement from an anonymous group called the GRPC Blues Busters (Glasgow Reformed Presbyterian Church). Other church leaders received similar encouragement. Thank-you notes to the Blues Busters started showing up in our church bulletin. Twenty-five years later, we do not know who those encouragers were, but their ministry served an ever-widening circle. Small groups in our church and other churches adopted this ministry when studying *Treasures of Encouragement*. What fun they had surprising nursery coordinators, music ministers, youth pastors, prison ministry counsellors, and so on. Use some of the ideas in this list of encouragement ideas. The *Treasures of Encouragement Leader's Guide* offers more ideas.

Appendix B

TREASURES OF ENCOURAGEMENT OVER THE YEARS

Encouragement Principle 1: God keeps His promises through other believers.

Thirty days after a diagnosis of breast cancer, I tackled my first round of chemo, followed by radiation and surgery. I faced not only fighting cancer but also moving our four children across the country to Alaska, where my husband was deployed. As a military wife I've always prided myself on my ability to handle every situation, but these circumstances were completely out of my league. As my body coped with a first dose of chemo, my thoughts ran to the unknown. How could I go through this in a strange place and still care for my four children and husband? God heard my cries and kept His promises through other believers, some whom I didn't know at all, others whom I didn't know very well: people I passed in church, colleagues of my husband, Sean; parents of the children on my kids' swim team. Twice a month my mother flew to Alaska for a week to give me time to recover and to prepare for the next treatment. God encircled me with people to encourage, support, and meet practical needs rather than leaving me alone. Even more gratifying is that in my weakness, I learned that God used me and my situation to encourage others. *Carrie McGaughan*

Encouragement Principle 2: We can be God's promise keepers by giving to others from the riches of our inheritance.

These past several years our family experienced life-changing trials that threatened to paralyze me with what-ifs. The life lessons I learned so long ago from *Treasures of Encouragement* helped to keep me grounded and reminded me to depend on the Scriptures to teach me how to respond based on what I know to be God's truth and not on how I feel. I am a "fixer," but there was no easy fix for the multiple family crises. This quote from the book comforted me, "Biblical encouragers know that their role is part of a process; it is seldom, if ever, the solution. . . . If . . . we respond purely on the basis of how we feel rather than on what we know, we will tend to look for ways to eliminate hurt rather than for ways to act as the arms and hands of God to uphold the hurting person while God accomplishes His purposes through the adversity" (pg. 73). Though it is often painful to watch loved ones struggle, I am grateful for the privilege to offer them treasures from the richness of my spiritual inheritance. *Barbara L'Italien*

Encouragement Principle 3: Encouragement is contagious.

Four years into a church planting ministry, our young congregation was still meeting in an elementary school cafeteria. My pastor husband asked me to do some teaching and training for the women at the same time as he trained elders and deacons. So, twenty-five years ago, as a young and inexperienced pastor's wife, I chose *Treasures of Encouragement* to begin implementing a ministry of encouragement. We did not know how soon we would need to live out the principles we were learning. Within just a few months, a young husband and father died in a car accident, leaving his wife and nine-month-old son. Our congregation lived out the Encouragement Principles as they surrounded this grieving family. They cared for the young widow out of God's care for them and provided meals, babysitting, notes, and much more. The older women walked closely beside her as she grieved. Each intentional act helped to turn her toward God's heart. I will never forget watching as what we had learned was lived out in a real situation. I am confident that the ministry of encouragement helped her to heal and to move forward in her life in a healthy way. *Sherry Kendrick*

Encouragement Principle 4: We revive village life when we take responsibility for one another.

Hearing that my athletic fourteen-year-old son was going to lose his lower right leg after a freak accident in West Africa sent me into a tailspin. Tears, faith questions, and intense sorrow filled the days, weeks, and months surrounding my son's amputation and recovery. How could such a devasting accident happen while we were serving as missionaries? Despite my heaviness and heartache, the Lord showed me He does indeed give treasures of comfort in the wilderness of crisis and loss. He showed my family His treasures of care through His body, the church—through meals, visits, cards, gifts, and so on. And He showed me treasures of His love through several friends who willingly entered into my pain. They walked with me in the suffering and did not leave me alone. Instead, they made time to visit with me, did not flinch when they heard my questions, and gave me the freedom and space I needed to process and heal. They pointed my heart to gospel truth and reminded me of the Lord's promises. Truly, God kept His promises of comfort and presence in the wilderness of suffering through these friends, His promise keepers. *Karen Weaver*

Encouragement Principle 5: The directing force behind encouragement is God's Word.

The mostly single and career-minded women in our New York City church questioned how a book written by a pastor's wife and grieving mother could benefit them. As we dove into *Treasures of Encouragement*, the women thrived and so did I. We learned how contagious and life-changing encouragement can be, especially when it is directed by God's Word. During this period I experienced several losses and questioned my worth and even my identity. Rejection and a sense of failure tempted me to focus only on what I could not do, not on Whose I was. I highlighted, underlined, and scribbled notes in the margin of this quote: "Circumstances do not change who you are. Your primary calling is to reflect the character and nature of God. Whether you are experiencing pain or prosperity, you have many treasures to offer people. When God calls you to offer the treasures of your inheritance, you are on holy ground. He is doing 'soul work' and He is giving you the privilege of fulfilling His promises in a needy heart. This is grace" (pg. 37). Thinking biblically about my identity reminded me that no matter my circumstances, I have the privilege of giving others the gift of encouragement. Yes, this is grace. *Dianne Balch*

Encouragement Principle 6: Biblical encouragement creates a loving community that causes others to glorify God.

Unexpected and unwanted drastic changes, sovereignly ordained by God, forced me to sell and get rid of my belongings in preparation for moving from a 5,500 square-foot house into a 1,300 square-foot home, an overwhelming task in the midst of deep pain. Imagine my relief when my friend texted on numerous mornings, "I'll be at your house at 9:00 a.m." Our friendship deepened as we sorted, packed, cried, laughed, and schlepped things to Goodwill. Another friend showed up at my door with spiral index cards. She had already written verses on fifteen of the cards and encouraged me to fill in other verses as I faced this journey of pain. Each time I received a verse by text, email, or card, I wrote it out. These cards are like a memorial stone, reminding me of God's unfailing love and comfort for me. He continues to keep His promises through my friends who pray with and for me, check in on me, and encourage me in my faith. These friends took responsibility for pointing me to Jesus during very dark days and by doing so, the darkness quickly became light because I could see hope from the Lord. *Kathy Wargo*

Encouragement Principle 7: Biblical encouragement builds confidence and results in increased ministry opportunities.

When Karen, the women's coordinator of our denomination's women's ministry, asked me to serve on the national team, I concluded she had dialed the wrong number. Frankly, her invitation scared me. I knew nothing about how to strategize and break new ground in women's ministry across the world, build relationships with women I had never met, or work with her team—which I hadn't even known existed. Why would I do this? Karen's response reminded me of my theology: serving God's church is a privilege and a blessing. How could I refuse? Karen's consistent mentoring of our team showed me how to be that same nurturing presence for others. Her encouragement built our confidence in the Lord, and the outreach grew beyond our expectations. I had a front-row seat as the Lord created an ever-widening circle of ministry, starting with this small group. He made good on her guarantee that this work would be a blessing and a privilege, but it was so much more because I saw His strength over and over again in my weakness. Thanks to Karen's encouragement, God increased my confidence in Him through the opportunity to minister to others. *Jane Anne Wilson*

Encouragement Principle 8: Through biblical encouragement we become spiritual mothers who leave a legacy of hope and courage.

I met my spiritual mother the day I enrolled my not-so-cooperative one-year-old daughter in the preschool Sherry oversaw. This fortysomething woman recognized my immature faith and longing to grow into my role as a Christian wife and mother. Sherry gently and slowly invited me into her life, where I learned how to love not just my family but others like me. The way she loved equipped me to patiently walk alongside a struggling person and to enter into their hurts and joys. She encouraged me to teach Sunday school, knowing I would learn foundational biblical truths along with the children. Then she prompted me to lead a little girls' ministry with her. When the adult women's ministry studied *Treasures of Encouragement*, we adapted the book for these elementary-school girls. Once more, service to our church family's little ones became a vehicle for me to better understand my God-given purpose and role. Now I am a grandmother and college nursing professor. It's a privilege to pass on to my family, students, and colleagues life lessons learned from my spiritual mother, Sherry. Our friendship truly is evidence that through biblical encouragement we become spiritual mothers who leave a legacy of hope and courage. *Heiddy DiGregorio*

Encouragement Principle 9: Consistent, fervent prayer is the greatest treasure of encouragement we have to offer.

My dying friend, Jean, though wracked with pain, whispered one word to me as I sat by her bed, knowing this might be the last time we talked: "Pray." Her marching orders reminded me of how she exemplified the preciousness of the gift of prayer. As a military wife and mother of eight, I was no stranger to stress and to handling crises during deployments. I learned to take advantage of alone time to pour out my heart to my heavenly Father. Prayer transformed my car into a sanctuary where only He heard my cries for wisdom and comfort in the solitude of running errands and in between chauffeuring my children. This particular morning, a song on the radio touched my heavy heart as I tearfully prayed for my daughter. I wiped my eyes after parking my car, looked up and saw Jean, my dear praying friend. I went to her. We hugged, and she asked what was wrong. All I could answer was, "My daughter." She responded, "I will pray." When the Lord placed my dear sister in that parking lot at the exact moment of my need, He gave me the priceless gift of prayer. Cancer won the battle in Jean's body, but her legacy lives on as I remember and accept her whispered marching orders to pray. My heart's desire is to give others the priceless gift of consistent, fervent prayer too. *Roberta Dosa*

Encouragement Principle 10: Biblical encouragement is like "apples of gold in settings of silver."

The doctors diagnosed my forty-seven-year-old husband with a cancerous brain tumor. The night we got the news, I received countless texts from friends and family. In the days following, many visited and prayed aloud, crying out to God for comfort and peace. Their sorrowful words and disbelief, prayers for wisdom, and Scripture were life-giving and a balm to my aching soul. Knowing others were stunned and grieving with us gave me freedom to share my own feelings of shock and utter sadness—not only with them but also with the Lord. Hearing others beseech the Lord on our behalf in the midst of their own pain reminded me God was near to us—His broken-hearted children—listening, caring, and loving. Words like "Scott will be okay" or "The Lord can heal him" did not comfort me. I knew my hope wasn't in Scott's healing. Rather, the words "We are hurting with you" and "Let me pray for you right now" were like apples of gold in settings of silver. Those life-giving words reminded me we were not alone in our pain and grief. These words reminded me where our true peace and hope was found: in Jesus and the promise of heaven with Him. Never underestimate the power of your words that are rooted in Jesus. They give hope and hold up the arms of the weary. *Jill Brown*

Encouragement Principle 11: God gives treasures of comfort in the wilderness of crisis and loss.

After years of marital abuse, I moved back to my childhood home with only the clothes on my back. Months passed as I relearned how to think clearly and make decisions. But I did not walk this pathway alone. A grade-school friend still lived in my hometown. She encouraged me in tangible ways only the Lord could know I needed. Medical issues limited my work options so every penny went to bills. Somehow she knew just when I was close to running out of favorite skin products and gave me full size "samples," knowing I couldn't afford such luxuries. She helped me to start new friendships and get acclimated to a new community. Fifteen years earlier, my heart had broken when a close friend moved from the Northeast to my home state. Now I know her move was the Lord's gift for me, placing her close by. She met practical needs and gently helped me to make decisions, recognizing I needed time to recover from the wounds before I could think clearly or process how to move forward. A lifelong long-distance friend routinely called and sent texts and emails filled with Scripture. She cried and prayed with me. She repeatedly reminded me my identity is in Jesus, not the harsh indictments of my husband. The intentional actions of each encourager reminded me that God is sovereign and I can trust Him. Truly God does give treasures of encouragement in the wilderness of suffering. *Terri Paoli*

Encouragement Principle 12: God transforms the encouragement of ordinary people into extraordinary ministry.

I pray these stories inspire you to pursue the beauty of joy of being God's promise keeper in the lives of others.

INDEX OF SCRIPTURE

Sharon Betters is a nationally known conference and retreat speaker and the author of several books. She and her husband, Chuck, are the founders of MARKINC Ministries, a platform for distributing free resources of hope and help to suffering people.

Did you find this book helpful?
Consider leaving a review online.
The author appreciates your feedback!

Or write to P&R at editorial@prpbooks.com
with your comments. We'd love to hear from you.

Treasures of Encouragement

Leader's Guide

This Leader's Guide will help you guide your women into deeper intimacy with Christ and cultivate a compassionate community within your study group. It is the author's desire that your local church will experience a sense of deeper community because encouragement that starts in a small group is *contagious*!

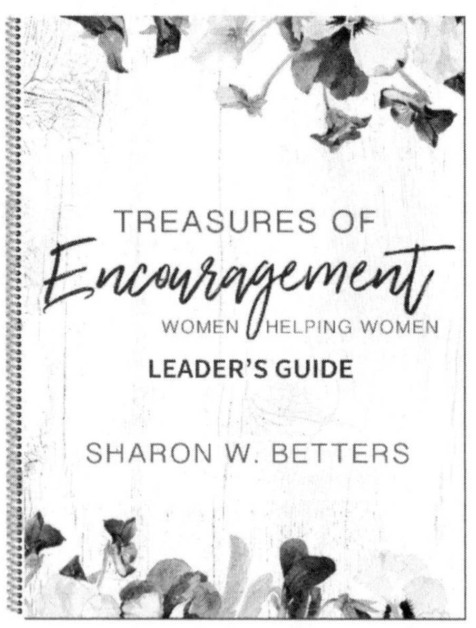

Available from the PCA Bookstore

www.pcabookstore.com

1.800.283.1357

MARKINC.org

Help, Hope & Healing

Scripture is clear that we will go through some sort of suffering...
Are you prepared?
MARKINC.org offers *free* resources to help you persevere by faith.

Redemptive stories addressing life's darkest circumstances that are often difficult to discuss, yet need to be faced as we help one another walk by faith. These are the real-life testimonies of people who have walked through similar experiences and have found their strength in Christ.

Daily *Treasure*

A 365 day devotional written by Sharon Betters and the occasional guest author, embraces the power of God's Word to encourage, equip and energize the reader to walk by faith in the pathway God has marked out for them, no matter how difficult. Each devotional includes a treasure from God's Word, life giving applications, guided prayers and a challenge to reflect God's love in a way that helps turn hearts toward Jesus.

Ask Dr. Betters

Q & A, topical video series where every week Dr. Chuck F. Betters answers tough questions on suffering and the sovereignty of God. Dr. Betters reinforces that God is good and worthy of our trust even when life is difficult and when we struggle to understand Him.

Online, Professional & Affordable.

Helps those hurting by anchoring their hope in Jesus by gaining a better understanding of His promises. We offer reputable, Biblical counseling services to people suffering or experiencing hard times, so that they might be better equipped to persevere by faith.

To learn more, please visit;

MARKINC.org

MORE FROM P&R PUBLISHING FOR YOUR ENCOURAGEMENT

The world pressures us to fulfill our desires—but God tells us to master them through contentment. This practical daily devotional helps us cultivate thankfulness in situations that fuel discontent.

In the 31-Day Devotionals for Life series, biblical counselors and Bible teachers guide you through Scripture passages that speak to specific situations or struggles, helping you to apply God's Word to your life in practical ways day after day.

Also in the 31-Day Devotionals for Life series:

Anger: Calming Your Heart, by Robert D. Jones
Anxiety: Knowing God's Peace, by Paul Tautges
Chronic Illness: Walking by Faith, by Esther Smith
Fearing Others: Putting God First, by Zach Schlegel
Forgiveness: Reflecting God's Mercy, by Hayley Satrom
Grief: Walking with Jesus, by Bob Kellemen
Marriage Conflict: Talking as Teammates, by Steve Hoppe
A Painful Past: Healing and Moving Forward, by Lauren Whitman
Pornography: Fighting for Purity, by Deepak Reju
Toxic Relationships: Taking Refuge in Christ, Ellen Mary Dykas